Printed in Canada
© Published and Copyrighted 2008 by
The Rohr Jewish Learning Institute
822 Eastern Parkway, Brooklyn, NY 11213

(888) YOUR-JLI/718-221-6900
www.myJLI.com

ב"ה

Soul maps

ספר לקוטי אמרים תניא

JLI

JEWISH LEARNING INSTITUTE

The **Rohr Jewish Learning Institute**
gratefully acknowledges
the pioneering support of

George and Pamela Rohr

SINCE ITS INCEPTION
the **Rohr JLI** has been
a beneficiary of the vision, generosity,
care and concern
of the **Rohr family**

In the merit of
the tens of thousands of hours of Torah study
by **JLI** students worldwide
may they be blessed with health,
Yiddishe Nachas from all their loved ones,
and extraordinary success
in all their endeavors

תְּנוּ לָהּ מִפְּרִי יָדֶיהָ וִיהַלְלוּהָ בַשְּׁעָרִים מַעֲשֶׂיהָ משלי לא,לא

This course is lovingly dedicated to the memory of

Mrs. Charlotte Rohr

on the occasion of her first *Yahrzeit*

י׳ מרחשון תשס״ט

MarCheshvan 10, 5769

לזכות האשה החשובה והיקרה

מרת **שרה** ע״ה

בת ר׳ יקותיאל יהודה ומרת לאה הי״ד

תנצב״ה

Endorsement for
Soul Maps

Rabbi Adin Even-Yisrael (Steinsaltz)

**ost moral works address** themselves to personal problems and to the ways that a person can attain specific goals in specific areas.

Tanya, by contrast, does not, in the main, address specific problems but delves into their root causes, seeking to distill the predicaments of humankind down to their most elementary maxims and to solve them in the most comprehensive way.

Tanya trains its students to see the many thousands of complexities, doubts, and drives within themselves as expressions of a single basic problem: the struggle between good and evil within the human soul.

Although the book is written with great restraint, it energetically and dramatically depicts life as an immense battle. This fight and our ability to conduct our lives within it are the very purpose of the creation of humankind. As *Tanya* explains it, this status is not simply the confrontation of good and evil, but rather the ongoing encounter between two components of the soul: the animal and the divine. The tension is between the part of the soul that draws us downward toward the earth and the part that aspires upward toward the divine.

The conflict, then, is not a war of annihilation in which man seeks to destroy certain parts of his soul, rather it is an effort to educate all parts of the human soul, to create within them a consciousness and a feeling—until their aspirations merge with those of the divine soul, so that the person reaches a state of perfect harmony between body and soul, between the earthly and the transcendent.

Rabbi Adin Even-Israel (Steinsaltz) is a scholar and social critic best known for his monumental translation of and commentary on the Talmud. He is also the founder of a worldwide network of Jewish educational institutions supported by The Aleph Society in the United States.

Table of Contents

ספר לקוטי אמרים תניא

Soul m a p s

Introduction to *Tanya*[1]

By **Rabbi Nissan Mindel, M.A., Ph.D.**

I. THE BOOK

The author called his work by three distinct names. Each of these names characterises the book in its own way. These names are:

1. *Likutei Amarim*—"Collected Discourses." By this name the author describes his work in his "Compiler's Foreword," thereby humbly disclaiming any originality for his work. In fact the author explicitly states that his treatise constitutes a collection of discourses, "which have been selected from books and scribes, heavenly saints, who are renowned among us."[2] Under this title the book was first published (Slavita, 1796).[3]

2. *Tanya,* after the initial word of the book, quoting a Baraitic source.[4] The quotation from tannaitic lore serves the author more than a homiletic introduction to his system. Dealing, as it does, with the mystic descent of the soul and its destiny, it provides the author with a starting point, based in the Talmud, from which to unfold his whole system. Under this title the book appeared for the second time (Zolkiev, 1798), with *Likutei Amarim* as subtitle.[5]

3. *Sefer shel Benonim*—"Book of the Intermediates," so called after the type of personality on which the book centers attention, that is, the intermediate type whose moral position is between the *tzaddik* ("righteous man") and *rasha* ("wicked man"). Thus the author pointedly indicates that

---

[1] Rabbi Shne'ur Zalman of Liadi, *Likutei Amarim (Tanya),* Introduction to first Bilingual Edition of *Tanya*, Kehot Publication Society (Brooklyn, NY, 1958).

[2] *Hakdamat ha-melaket* ("Compiler's Foreword"), *Ibid.*, p. 7.

[3] See list of 72 *Tanya* editions, *Ibid.*, pp. 427 ff.

[4] Niddah 30b.

[5] See footnote 3, above.

his primary concern is not with the *tzaddik,* upon whose veneration general *Chasidut* had placed so much emphasis, nor with the *rasha,* upon whose condemnation much has been said in other Jewish ethical works, but with the *benoni,* the "intermediate" man, whose rank is within reach of every person.[6] The name *Sefer shel Benonim* appeared as a subtitle in the first edition *("Likutei Amarim,* Part One, called *Sefer shel Benonim"*). However, actually the author often refers to the whole book, and not merely its first part, when using the title *Sefer shel Benonim.*[7]

The standard complete editions of this work include the following five parts, each of which is an independent treatise:

Part I: *Likutei Amarim,* or *Tanya,* or *Sefer shel Benonim,* proper, comprising a Foreword and fifty-three chapters (148 pp.).

Part II: *Sha'ar ha-Yichud veha-Emunah* ("Portal of Unity and Belief"), with a Foreword and twelve chapters (30 pp.).

Part III: *Igeret ha-Teshuvah* ("Epistle of Repentance"), with twelve chapters (22 pp.).

Part IV: *Igeret ha-Kodesh* ("Sacred Epistle"), with thirty-two sections (102 pp.).[8]

Part V: *Kuntress Acharon* ("Latest Treatise"), 20 pp.

Altogether at least sixty-five editions of the *Likutei Amarim,* or *Tanya,* complete or in part, have appeared to-date[9] with both names alternating as title and subtitle, respectively. Yet this work, as the other Chabad classics, has never been translated into any European language. Even in its Hebrew original it is not an easy book, because of its construction, almost complete lack of punctuation, and also because some of its basic doctrines are not treated fully therein and must be sought in the author's other works. There seems, therefore, ample reason for presenting to the English-speaking Jewish world a translation of this fundamental work of Chabad, with an introduction and notes, which it

---

[6] *Likutei Amarim (Tanya), op. cit.,* beg. ch. 14.

[7] *Ibid.,* p. 435.

[8] Parts IV and V, comprising epistles written by the author at different times and on various occasions, were incorporated by the author's sons.

[9] See footnote 3, above.

is hoped, will facilitate the comprehension of this book and its doctrine. Our present study will confine itself to Part I, to which we shall refer, for the sake of convenience, by its shorter name—*Tanya.*

The author worked on the *Tanya* for twenty years,[10] elaborating its style and form so punctiliously that it came to be regarded by his followers as the "Written Torah" of Chabad, where every word and letter was meaningful. Indeed, the author divided it into fifty-three chapters to correspond to the number of *Sidrot* (weekly portions) in the Pentateuch. It soon became the custom of many Chabad *chasidim* to study a chapter of the *Tanya* each week, with the same regularity with which the weekly portions of the Pentateuch were recited.[11]

In his attempt to design the *Tanya* so that it would meet the widest possible need, both of the analytical and searching mind, as well as of the less scholarly, the author has succeeded to a high degree. The former find in it an inexhaustible profundity, and several searching not yet published commentaries have been written on it. This translator has been fortunate in having access to some of the manuscripts in question.[12]

The less scholarly, too, each according to his intellectual capacity, find in it edifying instruction at varying levels. This quality, together with the authority it enjoys, accounts for the widespread recognition which the *Tanya* has commanded from the time of its appearance to the present day.

The *Tanya* was written, as the author indicates in his Foreword, for the "seekers" and the "perplexed." One is tempted to draw a parallel between this author and his book and Maimonides and his *Guide.* Indeed, both men present some striking points in common. Each of them first established his reputation as a Talmudist and Codifier before publishing a work of philosophy; both had written Codes of Jewish Law, which are still authoritative and popular. Each of them created a new lasting school of thought in Jewish philosophy, and the one, like

---

[10] Rabbi Menachem Mendel of Lubavitch, *Kitzurim VeHaorois LeTanya,* Rabbi Menachem M. Schneerson, ed. Kehot Publication Society (Brooklyn, N.Y., 1948), p. 121.

[11] *Ibid.,* pp. 123, 124.

[12] Two are by Rabbi Shmuel Grunem Esterman, first dean of the Yeshiva Tomchei Tmimim, founded in Lubavitch in 1897. A third, extant only in part, is believed to have been written by Rabbi Jacob Kadaner, a disciple of Rabbi Shne'ur Zalman's son and successor. A fourth commentary is of unknown origin.

the other, set out to write a work which aimed at helping those who needed guidance in their religious beliefs. Yet both of them evoked sharp opposition from the direction of a part of orthodox Jewry; both were misunderstood and their philosophical treatises were banned.

However, this is as far as the parallel goes. The *Guide* and the *Tanya* represent two widely divergent systems, in essence as well as in form. The two authors were separated by some six centuries in time, and far apart also geographically and in respect of the whole cultural milieu in which they flourished. Maimonides is the rational Jewish philosopher *par excellence;* Rabbi Shne'ur Zalman is basically a mystic. The "perplexed" for whom they wrote were two entirely different types of people. Maimonides wrote for the man whose perplexity derived from the fact that he desired to retain his traditional beliefs, but was puzzled by the apparent contradiction between tradition and philosophy, yet loath to give up either.[13] The object of the *Guide,* therefore, was to effect a reconciliation between the two.

No such problem confronted Rabbi Shne'ur Zalman. Philosophy and science hardly had a place among the masses of Eastern European Jewry at that time. The *Haskalah* movement had not yet made any serious inroads upon the minds of the masses. Rabbi Shne'ur Zalman addressed himself to those "who are in pursuit of righteousness and seek the Lord . . . whose intelligence and mind are confused and they wander about in darkness in the service of G-d, unable to perceive the beneficial light that is buried in books."[14] In other words, he writes for those whose beliefs have not been troubled by doubts, but who merely seek the right path to G-d.

We will, therefore, not find in the *Tanya* the type of scholastic philosophy with which the *Guide* is replete, nor any polemics, nor even an attempt to treat systematically many of the philosophical problems which engaged Maimonides' attention. Such basic beliefs as the Existence of G-d, *creatio ex nihilo,* Revelation, and others, are taken for granted by the author. Others, such as the Divine attributes, Providence, Unity, Messianism, etc., are treated as integral parts of his ethical system, and illuminated by the light of Kabbalah.

---

[13] *The Guide For the Perplexed,* tr. M. Friedlander (London, 1942), Introduction, p. 2.
[14] *Tanya, Ibid.,* beg. *Hakdamat ha-melaket.*

The *Tanya* is essentially a work on Jewish religious ethics. The author is primarily concerned with the forces of good and evil in human nature and in the surrounding world, and his objective, as already pointed out, is to pave a new way to the *summum bonum.* He is aware, of course, of the existence of Hebrew literature dealing with the same subject. If he is impelled to write a new book, it is not, as he is careful to note, because of the shortcomings of the available works *per se,* but because the human mind is not equally receptive, nor equally responsive to, the same stimuli. The implication is that many works on Jewish philosophy and ethics were useful for their time and age, or for the specific groups for whom they were written. Now there was a need for a new approach (in the light of the chassidic doctrine), and for a "guide" that would command a universal appeal. However, the author realises that even this book, in parts at least, cannot be so simple as to be understood by all. Consequently he urges the more learned not to be misled by a sense of misplaced modesty, and not to withhold their knowledge from those who would seek it from them in the understanding of these "Discourses."[15]

R. Shne'ur Zalman knew his "perplexed" intimately. They flocked to him in great numbers, and they flooded him with written inquiries. Most of them, undoubtedly, were simple folk and laymen. But there were also many students of the Talmud, and philosophically inclined young men, who, like himself in his teens, sought a new way of life and new outlets for their intellectual as well as spiritual drives. The consideration of such a variegated audience largely determined the form and style of the book.

Speaking of form and style, it should also be remembered that long before he committed his teachings and doctrines to writing, he preached them orally.[16] His sermons and discourses, delivered mostly on the Sabbath and on Festivals (which accounts for their homiletic style), were subsequently recorded from memory by his disciples. These manuscripts had a wide circulation among his followers. Not infrequently Rabbi Shne'ur Zalman expounded his doctrines in the form of epistles which, being of general interest, were regarded by his followers as pastoral letters, and also copied and recopied for the widest possible circulation.

---

[15] *Ibid.,* p. 7.

[16] Rabbi Shne'ur Zalman is said to have preached his doctrines orally for twelve years before committing them to writing. Comp., *Kitzurim, op. cit.,* p. 136.

In the course of time, as his community of devotees had greatly increased, Shne'ur Zalman felt, as he explains in his Foreword, that the time was ripe to present an outline of his teachings in the form of a book, which was to supersede the circulating pamphlets, many of which were replete with errors as a result of repeated copying and transcription, or by the malicious mischief of opponents.[17] This is how the *Likutei Amarim,* or *Tanya,* in its present composition, was born.

2. THE SOURCES

We have already noted that the author of the *Tanya* made no claim to originality for his work. On the contrary, he emphasised his dependence on his predecessors. Among the "books and sages" which influenced his thinking, the Scriptures, Talmud and Lurianic Kabbalah must be given foremost place. This is indicated already in the first chapter, which opens the book with Talmudic quotations, references to the Zoharitic literature and R. Chayyim Vital, the great exponent of Lurianic Kabbalah, and with interspersed quotations from Scripture. Here we already have an indication of the author's cast of mind and his aim to build his system on the combined foundations of Scriptural, Rabbinic and Kabbalistic sources.

Rabbi Shne'ur Zalman's interpretations and doctrines are based upon the teachings of the Ba'al Shem Tov, the founder of general *Chasidut,* and his own "masters," Rabbi Dov Ber of Miezricz, the Ba'al Shem Tov's successor, and Rabbi Dov Ber's son Rabbi Abraham, the "Angel."

The author draws abundantly from the *Zohar* and the *Tikunei Zohar.* He mentions by name Maimonides (the *Code of Jewish Law*), and Rabbi Moshe Cordovero *(Pardes).* Of other "books and scribes" which influenced him, though he does not mention them by name in the *Tanya,* are R. Isaiah Hurwitz's *Shnei Luchot Haberit,* the works of the Maharal (Rabbi Judah Lowe) of Prague, and Bachya ben Asher's *Commentary* on the Bible.[18]

---

[17] *Ibid.,* pp. 137, 139.

[18] The *Zohar is* mentioned in the *Tanya* (part I) forty-nine times; Luria—ten times; Vital and his works—twenty-nine times; Maimonides (Code of Jewish Law)—five times; Nachmanides—once. *Comp.,* "Index of Books and Persons" in *Tanya, op. cit.,* p. 398 ff.

Halevi's *Kuzari* was held in high esteem by Rabbi Shne'ur Zalman and his successors. He is known to have studied it ardently with his son and grandson who succeeded him. Similarly Bachya ibn Pakuda's *Duties of the Heart,* which enjoyed great popularity among Talmudic scholars of the day, as it still does.[19] Albo's *Ikarim* was another popular source for the philosophically inclined. It is safe to assume that Rabbi Shne'ur Zalman was intimately familiar with these, and no doubt also with the whole range of Medieval Jewish philosophy, but there is no evidence of influence by these sources on the composition of the *Tanya.*

It has been wisely said that the proper approach to a problem is in itself half a solution. Quite often it is the approach to the problem, and the method of treating it, that display the greatest degree of ingenuity and originality, and in themselves constitute the main contribution of the thinker. This is true of R. Shne'ur Zalman and of the Chabad system which he created. For, while his basic concepts have been gleaned from various sources, his doctrines nevertheless present a complete and unified system, and there is much refreshing originality in its presentation and consistency.

But R. Shne'ur Zalman did more than that. Very often he has so modified, reinterpreted or remolded the ideas which he had assimilated, as to give them an originality of their own.

To Rabbi Shne'ur Zalman, as to Kabbalists in general, the Torah, the Jewish Written and Oral Law embodied in the Bible and Talmud (the latter including both the Halachah and Aggadah), was more than a Divinely inspired guide to the *summum bonum.* It constituted the essential law and order of the created universe.[20] The Kabbalah, in its interpretation, was nothing but the inner, esoteric dimension of the Torah, its very "soul." Without this dimension the Torah could not be fully understood. Consequently, when he looked for the "inner," or esoteric, meaning of Biblical and Talmudic texts it was not for the

---

[19] Even where philosophical speculation was frowned upon, Bachya's *Duties of the Heart* enjoyed a unique position. The influential Rabbi Isaiah Hurwitz, for example, severely criticised in his work R. Abraham ibn Ezra, Maimonides (*Guide For The Perplexed*), and Gersonides, but held *Duties of the Heart* in high esteem. See *Shnei Luchot Haberit* (Amsterdam, 1698), pp. 2b; 8a; 20b; 47b; 183a; 193b.

[20] *Comp.,* "He looked into the Torah and created the world," *Zohar* (Vilna ["Rom" ed.], 1937), vol. II, 161a; vol. III, 35b, etc. See also, Tanchuma, at the beginning on Mishlei/Proverbs 8:30, to the effect that the Torah was the Divine "tool" in creating the universe.

purpose of adding homiletic poignancy to his exposition, but rather to reveal their inner dimension. In his system the esoteric and exoteric, the Kabbalah and the Talmud, are thoroughly blended and unified, just as the physical and metaphysical, the body and soul, emerge under his treatment as two aspects of the same thing. The polarity of things is but external; the underlying reality of everything is unity, reflecting the unity of the Creator. To bring out this unity of the microcosm and macrocosm, as they merge within the mystic unity of the *En Sof* (The Infinite)—that is the ultimate aim of his system.

3. THE COMPOSITION OF THE *TANYA*

Structurally, the *Tanya* may be divided into a number of sections, each dealing with a major subject and comprising a number of composite topics.

The first section of the work (chapters 1–8) is devoted to an analysis of the psychological structure of the Jewish personality.[21] Here the author discusses the two levels of consciousness (to use modern terminology) on which a person operates. These two levels of consciousness are derived from two sources, which the author terms the "divine soul" and the "animal soul." He examines the essential attributes and practical faculties of each. In dealing with the "animal soul" the author discusses also the nature of evil, both metaphysical and moral. Evil is basically conceived in terms of disunity; good in terms of unity.

Next (chapters 9–17), the author goes on to examine the inevitable conflict ensuing from the two divergent sources of consciousness. He evaluates the relative strength of the two souls and their respective functions, whereby the essential unity of the human personality is strongly upheld. Experientially, however, the conflict produces a variety of personalities, from one extreme to the other, which the author proceeds to define. His attention is focused on the

---

[21] With R. Isaiah Hurwitz and all Kabbalists, Rabbi Shne'ur Zalman considered the Jewish psychological composition in a category of its own. Judah Halevi made the special destiny of the Jewish people one of the basic doctrines of his *Kuzari.* In the *Tanya,* the emphasis is on the individual Jew rather than on the Jewish people as a whole.

personality of the *Benoni,* which falls mid-way between the extremes. However, in Rabbi Shne'ur Zalman's definition the *Benoni* is not one whose sins and virtues balance, while the *tzaddik* is a person whose good deeds outweigh his sins, as sometimes defined in the Talmud.[22] The *Benoni* of the *Tanya* is a person who exercises complete self-control and never commits a sin knowingly in any of the three areas of human activity: thought, speech and deed. The *Benoni* of the *Tanya* is thus superior to the *tzaddik* of the Talmud. Nevertheless, our author insists that this ideal personality is within grasp of the average individual, although not without constant effort and vigilance. The underlying doctrine here is that man is essentially and inherently a moral being.

The following chapters (18–25) are designed to support the author's basic theory, namely, that the ideal personality of the *Benoni* is not a mere concept, but one that can actually be realised. To this end he re-examines the functions of the soul, both on the conscious and subconscious level. With regard to the former, the author insists on the supremacy of the intellect. As for the subconscious level, the author draws upon the *Zohar* for certain mystical categories, such as the innate or "hidden" love and fear (awe) of G-d. The "hidden" love provides a subconscious urge for oneness with G-d; the sense of awe for the Divine Being provides a dread of separateness. Love and awe are therefore not conflicting, but rather complementary categories. The author emphasises the special, and to a considerable extent also hereditary, nature of the Jew, and his attachment to the idea of the unity of G-d, originating with the Patriarchs. This thought is, in some respects, strongly reminiscent of Halevi's concept of the "Divine Influence" *(al'amar al'ilahi),* which Halevi considers germane to the Jewish people.[23]

In this connection the doctrine of Divine Unity comes under discussion.

However, never losing sight of the practical, the author discusses certain states of mind which have a direct bearing on the quest for personal unity as a prelude to unity in the cosmic order, which in turn is *sine qua non* for the realisation of the Divine Unity. He offers a series of practical suggestions to attain mental and emotional stability and inner harmony. The emphasis is on joy, stemming

---

[22] Berachot 7a; Rosh Hashanah 16b. See discussion of this subject in first ch. of *Tanya, op. cit.*
[23] Rabbi Judah Halevi, *Kuzari,* 1:25, 27ff.

from an intellectually achieved faith, while sadness and dejection are severely censured. All this forms the subject matter of chapters 26–31.

Chapter 32 stands out by itself, as an interpolation not immediately related to the specific discussion. The careful student will note that chapter 31 is more directly continued in chapter 33. It would appear that the author chose to include this particular chapter parenthetically, as it were, in order to give emphasis at this point to one of the cardinal teachings of the Ba'al Shem Tov, which is a cornerstone of *Chasidut*, and which receives special attention in Chabad.[24] We refer to the subject of *ahavat yisrael,* love for fellow Jew (Vayikra/ Leviticus 18:19). In his familiar way, our author gives this precept a mystico- ethical exposition, based on the close soul-relationship within the community of Israel, to which he alluded in his Foreword and chapter 2, and which now receives fuller treatment in this chapter. Hence, some leading *chasidim* note the significance of the number of this chapter—32—corresponding to the Hebrew word *lev,* "heart."[25]

The drama of the inner personal conflict leads the author to an examination of man's destiny, the meaning and purpose of life, and man's place in the cosmic order. These problems are dealt with in chapters 33–37. In the last of these, the author outlines his concept of the Messianic Era and the Resurrection, when the cosmic order will have attained the acme of perfection and fulfillment as a direct result of man's conscious effort to work towards that goal.

At this point, the author might have concluded his treatise. However, he is not content with leaving us with the impression that life is merely a prelude to after-life. There must be more to life, and to religious experience than serv- ing merely as a means to an end. In the next, and last, fifteen chapters of his work, the author evolves his concept of the Kingdom of Heaven on earth in the *here and now.* In his daily life man is offered a foretaste of the after-life, and in some respects it is of a quality surpassing even the spiritual bliss of the hereafter. The author, therefore, takes up again those categories of man's

---

[24] *See, e.g.,* Rabbi Shne'ur Zalman of Liadi, *Likutei Torah* (Vilna ["Rom" ed.], 1928), Vol. I, Matot, pp. 85d ff.; R. Menachem Mendel of Lubavitch, *Derech Mitzvotecha,* Kehot Publication Society (Brooklyn, N.Y., 1953), pp. 28a ff., *et al.*

[25] I am indebted to Rabbi Menachem Schneerson, the Lubavitcher Rebbe, *shlita,* for calling my attention to the subject of this chapter.

spiritual phenomena which enable him to transcend his physical limitations and to partake of the supernatural in this life. Here again the mystic is very much in evidence. The author provides new insights into the concept of *kavanah* (the "intention" which must accompany every human act), which is the vehicle of transcendence (chapters 38–40). He discusses the various qualities of *fear (awe)* and love, and introduces also the quality of *mercy*, as the basic elements of this transcendency, and as innate qualities in human nature to leap over the gulf that separates the created from the Creator, and to come in direct contact with the *En Sof*, the Limitless (chapters 41–47).

The next two chapters (48–49) are devoted to the all-important Lurianic doctrine of *tzimtzum* which, in the author's system holds the key to both the mystery of creation and the destiny of man. Both man and the world in which he lives are two-dimensional creatures of matter and spirit. The tension that inheres in such an order can be relieved only by spiritualising the material. Man has it in his power to achieve personal harmony and unity, by realising his inner nature. In so doing, he becomes the instrument through which the world in which he lives also achieves fulfillment. To be a true master of the world which the Creator had entrusted in his hands, man must first be master of himself. Creation is seen as a process leading from G-d to man; fulfillment is seen as a process leading from man to G-d. The process leading from G-d to man is one of materialising the spiritual; that leading from man to G-d one of spiritualising the material. There is community of interests, as it were, between the Creator and His "counterpart" on earth, a community of interests which is realisable because of a community of "nature," since man partakes in the Divine nature (by reason of the fact that his soul is a "part" of G-dliness) as G-d concerns Himself with human affairs.

Man's moral acts must be holy acts.[26] The good and the holy are identical; man's duty and purpose in life is to identify himself with his Creator, through identifying his will with that of his Creator. Man is the Divine instrument "to make this world a fitting abode for the *Shechinah* (Divine Presence)," in which both man and G-d can share intimately and fully, in complete harmony and union. On this mystical note the final chapters (50–53) of the treatise conclude.

---

[26] *Comp., Shnei Luchot Haberit*, pp. 326b; 380b.

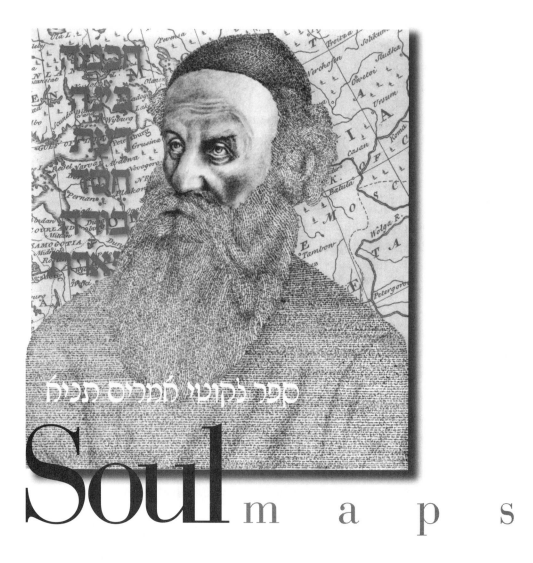

ספר לקוטי אמרים תניא

Soul maps

Lesson 1
Soul Words

Introduction

So you think you are perfect just the way you are . . . or you think the idea of perfection is a myth and an impossibility. You think humans are born in sin, or that we are all pure until the world gets its hands on us . . . .

Truth, of course, is always more nuanced. And the only absolute is that nothing is absolute. We will begin our inner journey with a revolutionary new look at the basic moral divide.

Hint: if you think we're going to be drawing the line between good and evil, you are in for a big surprise.

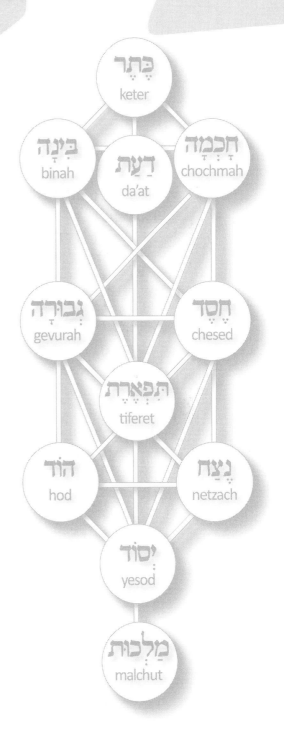

The World of *Tanya*
A Program, Not a Book

Text 1 ▮

אַךְ בְּיוֹדְעַיי וּמַכּירַיי קָאָמֵינָא . . .
אֲשֶׁר הָיָה הַדִּבּוּר שֶׁל חִיבָּה מָצוּי בֵּינֵינוּ
וְגִילּוּ לְפָנַי כָּל תַּעֲלוּמוֹת לִבָּם וּמוֹחָם בַּעֲבוֹדַת ה׳ הַתְּלוּיָה בַּלֵּב . . .
וְכוּלָּם הֵן תְּשׁוּבוֹת עַל שְׁאֵלוֹת רַבּוֹת אֲשֶׁר שׁוֹאֲלִין בְּעֵצָה כָּל אַנְ״שׁ . . .
תָּמִיד כָּל אֶחָד לְפִי עֶרְכּוֹ לָשִׂית עֵצוֹת בְּנַפְשָׁם בַּעֲבוֹדַת ה׳
לִהְיוֹת כִּי אֵין הַזְּמַן גַּרְמָא עוֹד
לְהָשִׁיב לְכָל אֶחָד וְאֶחָד עַל שְׁאֵלָתוֹ בִּפְרָטוּת וְגַם הַשִּׁכְחָה מְצוּיָה
עַל כֵּן רָשַׁמְתִּי כָּל הַתְּשׁוּבוֹת עַל כָּל הַשְּׁאֵלוֹת . . .
וְלֹא יִדְחַק עוֹד לִיכָּנֵס לְדַבֵּר עִמִּי בִּיחִידוּת
כִּי בָּהֶן יִמְצָא מַרְגּוֹעַ לְנַפְשׁוֹ וְעֵצָה נְכוֹנָה לְכָל דָּבָר הַקָּשֶׁה עָלָיו בַּעֲבוֹדַת ה׳

הקדמת המלקט

I address those who know me well . . . with whom affectionate words were often exchanged in private audience and who revealed to me all the hidden recesses of their hearts and minds in matters related to the service of G-d . . . .

All of these compiled sayings are answers to many questions posed continually by our fellows . . . seeking advice, each according to their stature in the service of G-d, so as to receive guidance for themselves in the service of G-d.

Because time no longer permits me to reply to everyone individually on his particular query, and also because [the advice heard in private audience] may be forgotten, I have recorded all the replies to all the questions . . . .

No longer will [they] need to press for a private audience, for in these *Likutei Amarim*/Collected Discourses [they] will find tranquillity for [their] souls and true counsel on everything that [they] find difficult in the service of G-d.

TANYA, COMPILER'S FOREWORD

Question for Discussion

Think of an area in which you are skilled, whether sports, music, a hobby, or a professional skill. How did you gain that skill?

Entering the World of *Tanya*

Learning Exercise 1

All of us regularly make resolutions, whether they are New Year's resolutions, birthday resolutions, or just plain "It's time to take charge of my life" resolutions. We decide that we would like to be a certain way, and we need to change our behavior to achieve that goal.

Yet often, a few days or a few months or a few years later, we find that we have not followed through.

1. For the purpose of this exercise, think of one failed resolution that you have made. Write it down.

2. Now think about why you did not follow through on that resolution. Write it down.

What is it that you really want—to follow through on that resolution, or to abandon the resolution?

Which "you" is the real "you"?

"Two Souls" Doctrine
The Animal Soul

Text 2

דלכל איש ישראל אחד צדיק ואחד רשע יש שתי נשמות
דכתיב "ונשמות אני עשיתי"
שהן שתי נפשות נפש אחת מצד הקליפה וסטרא אחרא
והיא המתלבשת בדם האדם להחיות הגוף
וכדכתיב "כי נפש הבשר בדם היא"
וממנה באות כל המדות רעות
וגם מדות טובות שבטבע כל ישראל . . .
כי בישראל נפש זו דקליפה היא מקליפ' נוגה שיש בה גם כן טוב

Every Jew [irrespective of his or her spiritual standing] possesses two souls, as it is written, "And *neshamot* (souls) I have made (Yeshayahu/ Isaiah 57:16)". These are two souls. One originates in non-holiness and this is the soul that is clothed in the blood of a human being to give life to the body; as it is written, "For the soul of the flesh is in the blood (Vayikra/Leviticus 17:11)." . . . . From [this soul] stems all of the evil, as well as the naturally good traits, for this soul of non-holiness is derived from a neutral level of non-holiness which also contains good.

TANYA, CHAPTER 1

The G-dly Soul

Text 3 📜

ונפש השנית בישראל היא חלק אלו-ה ממעל ממש
כמו שכתוב "ויפח באפיו נשמת חיים" "ואתה נפחת בי"
וכמ"ש בזוהר "מאן דנפח מתוכיה נפח" פי' מתוכיותו ומפנימיותו
שתוכיות ופנימיות החיות שבאדם מוציא בנפיחתו בכח

But the second soul of the Jew is truly "a part of G-d above," as it is written concerning Adam, "And [G-d] breathed into his nostrils a soul of life," and [as we say in the morning prayers] "You breathed [my soul] into me." It is written in the *Zohar*, "When one exhales, he exhales from [deep] within him." That is, he exhales from his innermost being, for it is of his innermost vitality that a person emits through exhaling with force.

TANYA, CHAPTER 2

מאן דנפח מתוכיה נפח

Contrasting the Two Souls
Learning Exercise 2

Place each of these pairs of words into the chart below, so that each column describes one of the souls and each row represents a contrasting quality of the two souls:

Selfish
Altruistic
"Breathed" into us
Embodied in the blood
Seeks pleasure
Seeks G-dliness
Primal Soul
"Second" Soul
Relates to the Transcendent
Relates to the Natural

Table 1: The Two Souls

Animal Soul	**G-dly** Soul

Structure of the Souls

Structure of the G-dly Soul

Text 4 ▦

והנה כל בחי׳ ומדרגה משלש אלו נפש רוח ונשמה
כלולה מעשר בחי׳ כנגד עשר ספירות עליונות שנשתלשלו מהן

The soul consists of ten faculties corresponding to the Ten Supernal *Sefirot* from which they derive.

TANYA, CHAPTER 3

Figure 1: Sefirot—Faculties of the Soul

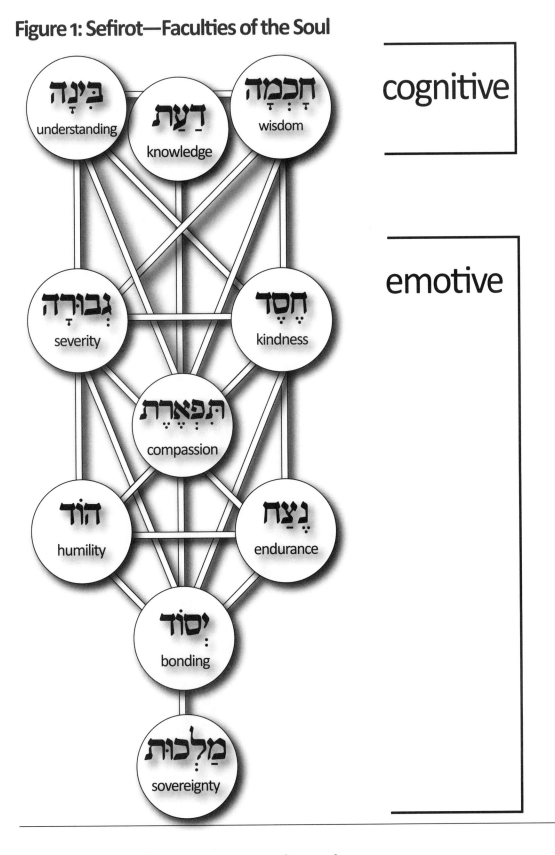

בִּינָה
understanding

דַּעַת
knowledge

חָכְמָה
wisdom

cognitive

גְּבוּרָה
severity

חֶסֶד
kindness

emotive

תִּפְאֶרֶת
compassion

הוֹד
humility

נֶצַח
endurance

יְסוֹד
bonding

מַלְכוּת
sovereignty

Garments of the G-dly Soul

Text 5

וְעוֹד יֵשׁ לְכָל נֶפֶשׁ אֱלֹקִית שְׁלֹשָׁה לְבוּשִׁים
שֶׁהֵם מַחֲשָׁבָה דִבּוּר וּמַעֲשֶׂה שֶׁל תרי״ג מִצְוֹת הַתּוֹרָה

I n addition [to its ten faculties], every G-dly soul possesses three garments. They are: thought, speech, and action as they find expression in the 613 commandments of the Torah.

TANYA, CHAPTER 4

מחשבה
דבור
מעשה

Figure 2:
The Ten Faculties and the Three Garments of the Soul

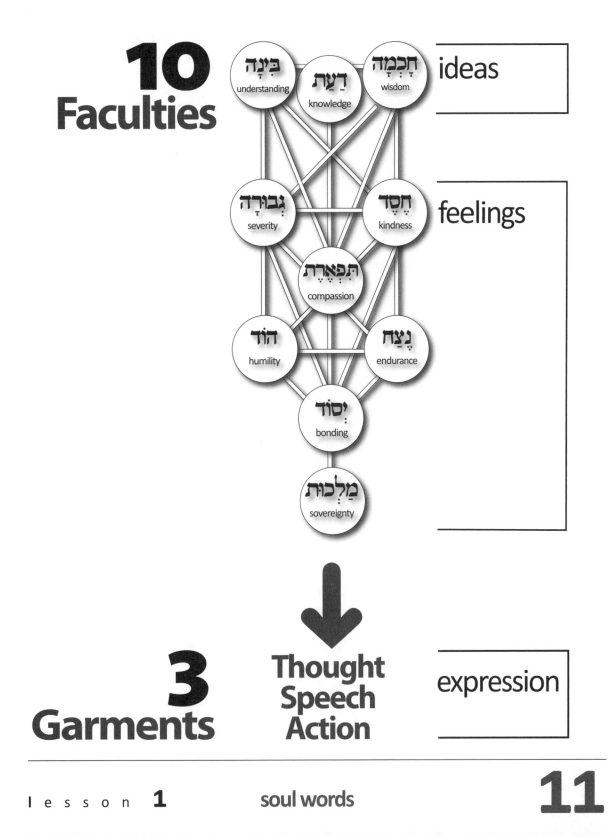

10
Faculties

בִּינָה
understanding

דַעַת
knowledge

חָכְמָה
wisdom

ideas

גְּבוּרָה
severity

חֶסֶד
kindness

feelings

תִּפְאֶרֶת
compassion

הוֹד
humility

נֶצַח
endurance

יְסוֹד
bonding

מַלְכוּת
sovereignty

3
Garments

Thought
Speech
Action

expression

Table 2

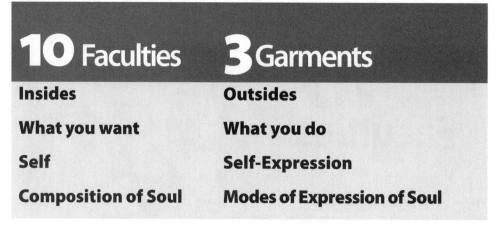

10 Faculties	**3** Garments
Insides	Outsides
What you want	What you do
Self	Self-Expression
Composition of Soul	Modes of Expression of Soul

Structure and Garments of the Animal Soul

Text 6

והנה זה לעומת זה עשה אלקים
כי כמו שנפש האלקית כלולה מעשר ספירות קדושות
ומתלבשת בשלשה לבושים קדושים
כך הנפש דסטרא אחרא מקליפות נוגה המלובשת בדם האדם
כלולה מעשר כתרין דמסאבותא

"The Almighty has created one thing opposite the other (Kohelet/Ecclesiastes 7:14)." Just as the G-dly soul consists of ten holy faculties, which correspond to the Ten Supernal *Sefirot*, and [the soul] is clothed in three holy garments, so too, the non-holy soul which is clothed in man's blood, consists of ten "crowns of impurity."

TANYA, CHAPTER 6

Text 7

כשאדם מחשב בהן או מדבר או עושה
הרי מחשבתו שבמוחו
ודבורו שבפיו
וכח המעשיי שבידיו ושאר איבריו
נקראים לבושי מסאבו לעשר בחי' אלו הטמאות
שמתלבשות בהן בשעת מעשה או דבור או מחשבה

When a person thinks [thoughts originating from the intelligence and emotions of the animal soul] or speaks words originating from them or does an act which serves or expresses them, then the thought in his brain, the words in his mouth and the power of action in his hands and other organs, are called "impure garments," for these ten unclean categories [i.e., the intelligence and emotions of the animal soul] clothe themselves in these garments during the time of that action, speech, or thought.

TANYA, CHAPTER 6

Table 3

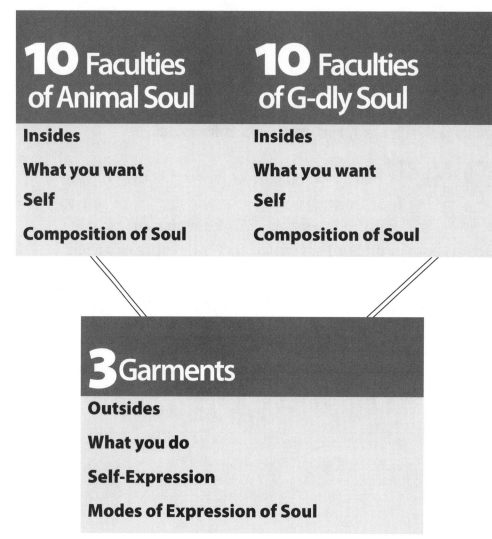

10 Faculties of Animal Soul

Insides

What you want

Self

Composition of Soul

10 Faculties of G-dly Soul

Insides

What you want

Self

Composition of Soul

3 Garments

Outsides

What you do

Self-Expression

Modes of Expression of Soul

Learning Exercise 3

Let's say I bet you a million dollars that you could not give up your favorite food for a year. If you manage to resist this food, at the end of the year, you become a millionaire. If you succumb to temptation even once, however, you need to give me a million dollars.

Will you take the bet?

Now imagine that I bet you a million dollars that you can't make yourself hate the food within a year's time. In a year, I give you a lie-detector test, and if you cannot truthfully answer that you hate the food, you will owe me one million dollars. Will you accept the second bet?

If you answered differently regarding the two bets, explain briefly what the difference is between the two.

Text 8

וכן כל הדבורים וכל המחשבות . . .
אשר לא לה׳ המה ולרצונו ולעבודתו
שזהו פי׳ לשון סטרא אחרא
פי׳ צד אחר שאינו צד הקדושה וצד הקדושה

Deeds . . . . words and thoughts that are not directed to G-d, to His Will and His service, are all garments for the animal soul. For this is the meaning of the term *sitra achra*—literally "the other side," i.e., [anything that is] *not* on the side of holiness.

TANYA, CHAPTER 6

Negotiating the "Gray Area"
Neutral Non-holiness

Text 9 🔖

אלא שהקליפות הן נחלקות לשתי מדרגות זו למטה מזו
המדרגה התחתונה היא שלש קליפות הטמאות
ורעות לגמרי ואין בהם טוב כלל

The category of non-holiness is divided into two categories, one lower than the other. The lower category consists of that which is completely impure and evil, containing no good whatever.

TANYA, CHAPTER 6

Text 10

ד״מ [דרך משל] האוכל בשרא שמינא דתורא ושותה יין מבושם
להרחיב דעתו לה׳ ולתורתו כדאמר רבא חמרא וריחא כו׳
או בשביל כדי לקיים מצות ענג שבת וי״ט
אזי נתברר חיות הבשר והיין שהיה נשפע מקליפת נוגה ועולה לה׳ כעולה וכקרבן
וכן האומר מילתא דבדיחותא
לפקח דעתו ולשמח לבו לה׳ ולתורתו ועבודתו שצריכים להיות בשמחה
וכמו שעשה רבא לתלמידיו
שאמר לפניהם מילתא דבדיחותא תחלה ובדחי רבנן

or instance, if one eats [delicacies like] fat beef and drinks spiced wine in order to broaden his mind for the service of G-d and for His Torah—as Rava said, "Wine and fragrance [make my mind more receptive],"—or in order to fulfill the commandment to enjoy the Sabbath and the festivals so, too, concerning speech. For example, he who makes a humorous remark to sharpen his mind and make his heart rejoice in G-d and His Torah and service, which should be practiced joyfully—as Rava was wont to do with his pupils, prefacing his discourse with a humorous remark, whereupon the students became cheerful.

TANYA, CHAPTER 7

The Three Utterly Unclean *Kelipot*

Text 11

שזהו לשון היתר ומותר

כלומר שאינו קשור ואסור בידי החיצונים שלא יוכל לחזור ולעלות לה'...

מה שאין כן במאכלות אסורות וביאות אסורות

שהן משלש קליפות הטמאות לגמרי

הם אסורים וקשורים בידי החיצונים לעולם

The terms *heter* (permissibility) and *mutar* (permissible) imply that which is not "tied down" . . . from ascending to G-d.

Such is not the case with [those things which are] forbidden, which are derived from the level of abject unholiness. They are tied down forever.

TANYA, CHAPTER 7

Figure 3: Maslow's Hierarchy of Needs

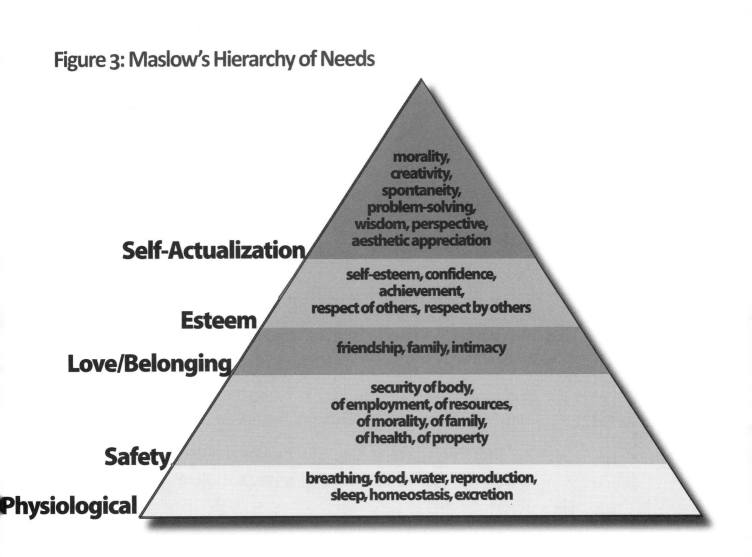

Learning Exercise 4

1. Look carefully at the hierarchy of needs and desires in this diagram. Where on the hierarchy would you place the cutoff between the desires of the animal soul and the desires of the G-dly soul?

2. Look carefully at the hierarchy of needs and desires in this diagram. Which of these pursuits can become holy pursuits? Which are inherently unholy pursuits?

Key Points

1. We have two souls: an animal soul and a G-dly soul.

2. The animal soul is selfish and concerned primarily with self-preservation, while the G-dly soul is selfless and concerned with G-dliness.

3. Each soul has ten faculties: three cognitive and seven emotive capacities, mirroring the ten *sefirot*.

4. There are three garments of external expression: thought, speech, and action.

5. The animal soul is rooted in *kelipat nogah* (neutral non-holiness) which has the potential to be elevated to holiness.

6. The three utterly unclean *kelipot*, however, are eternally irredeemable and cannot be elevated to holiness.

Additional Readings

Spicy Food

by **Rabbi Yanki Tauber**

One day, about 200 years ago, there was a fire in hell. The whole place burned down. It was bound to happen sooner or later, with those infernal fires burning night and day and the old devils getting careless over the years.

So they called in a troop of architects, contractors and interior designers and built a brand new gehenna. They redid the whole thing, from the landscaping to the ceramic in the bathrooms. But then the righteous folk upstairs in heaven started complaining. "The wicked guys get a new, modern complex, while we're housed in this 5000-year-old dilapidated place? Is this heaven's idea of justice?" It was decided that the righteous were right. The wicked were relocated to the old paradise, which now became the new hell; and the holy folk moved into the old gehenna, which became the new heaven.

Chassidim used to tell this story to illustrate what happened when the founder of Chabad Chassidism, Rabbi Schneur Zalman of Liadi, published his *Tanya* in 1796.

On the cover page of *Tanya*, the author states that he is saying nothing new; all this book is, Rabbi Schneur Zalman insists, is a "collection of sayings" by authors and teachers of Torah of previous generations. Indeed, everything stated in *Tanya* can be found in earlier sources. But as collected and presented by Rabbi Schneur Zalman, they constitute nothing less than a revolutionary understanding of our inner self and our purpose in life.

Before the *Tanya*, the human condition was a spiritual hell. It was a place of dissonance, self-doubt and, above all, a crushing sense of futility over the never-ending conflict between instinct and understanding. Why is it—the typical human asked him/herself a hundred times a day—that I desire things I don't want to desire? That I need to force myself to do what I've already decided I want to do? That I'm attracted to things that revolt me, and shy away from things I consider good and desirable? Am I such a weak and confused creature that I don't know my own mind and cannot act on my own convictions?

Before the *Tanya*, the typical human being often felt as if there were not one, but two selves residing within his or her body: a lower self that lusts and obsesses and grabs and greeds; and a higher self that commits and shares and is capable of awe and makes space in itself for higher truths. The typical human being yearned for tranquility, for inner quiet, for a resolution of the unending struggle within his fragmented heart. But the yearned-for tranquility never came.

In *Tanya*, Rabbi Schneur Zalman affirmed: yes, there are two selves inside us, and yes, they are engaged in constant battle over control of our lives. We each posses a self-focused "animal soul" which instinctively desires and craves that which preserves, nourishes, enhances and perpetuates itself. And we each have at our core an upward-focused "G-dly soul" that is aware of its source in G-dand strives to reunite with it as a spark craves to be absorbed in the great fire from which it emerged. Our every action, word and thought, our every motive, craving and desire, is an outcome of this ongoing battle within our hearts.

And then Rabbi Schneur Zalman drops his bombshell: this struggle, these conflicting desires, this confusion and self-doubt and inner turmoil, is not a spiritual hell. It is a spiritual heaven.

Indeed, says the *Tanya*, there do exist perfectly righteous individuals—called *tzaddikim*—who have resolved the conflict, whose two souls strive in harmony, whose "selfish" self has been trained and sublimated and brought in sync with their G-dly self. But these individuals are few and far between—a handful in each generation, perhaps a handful in the history of humankind. The rest of us are what Rabbi Schneur Zalman terms *beinonim* ("intermediates")—typical human beings. The rest of us are spiritual warriors, whose calling in life is to fight the battle with integrity, with gusto and with joy.

Why are there *tzaddikim* and *beinonim*? Because G-d desires both:

There are two types of pleasure before G-d. The first is from the complete nullification of evil and its transformation from bitterness to sweetness and from darkness to light by the perfectly righteous. The second [pleasure] is when evil is repelled while it is still at its strongest and mightiest . . . through the efforts of the *beinoni*. . . . As in the analogy of physical food, in which there are two types of delicacies that give pleasure: the first being the pleasure derived from sweet and pleasant foods; and the second, from tart and sour foods, which are spiced and prepared in such a way that they become delicacies that revive the soul . . . . (*Tanya*, ch. 27)

If your inner life is tranquil, if no demons plague your thoughts and no dichotomies rend your being, then one of two things are true: either you are a *tzaddik*, or else you are a *beinoni* who abandoned the battlefield. So unless you are so supercilious as to consider yourself a perfectly righteous *tzaddik*, this inner quietude should greatly alarm you. For what meaning, significance and joy can there be in a life that brings no pleasure to G-d?

Once upon a time, there was a heaven and a hell. Then, one day about two hundred years ago, the old heaven became the new hell, and the old hell was refurbished as the new heaven.

Reprinted with permission from chabad.org

Man of War

By **Rabbi Adin Steinsaltz**

Since I began writing about the *Tanya*—Rabbi Schneur Zalman of Liadi's revolutionary work on Hasidut from the late 18th century—I have been asked many times about the connection of *Tanya* to Kabbalah.

First of all, one must be cautioned that, when speaking about Kabbalah, it does not refer to the numerous imitations being sold nowadays in the form of little booklets, red strings, and healing waters. All of these approaches take the name of Kabbalah in vain, for the utmost secrets of the world and the promise of eternal life, protective angels, and supreme devotion cannot be purchased for five cents apiece. This type of commercialized mysticism is surely more propagated today than authentic Kabbalah and has the dangerous ability to deceive the masses into believing that they have discovered the essence of Kabbalah.

Kabbalah is—or at least has been for the last 500 years— the official theology of the Jewish people. It is the route to gaining a better understanding of the relationship between man and God. Anyone who feels any sort of connection to God should have enough sense to be interested in knowing God. This is true about so many other things; for instance, if I love or admire somebody, I have a desire to know that person better and in a deeper, more intimate way.

As a genre of literature, *Tanya* is what one may call "applied Kabbalah." It is not a pure theological statement or part of the theology itself; rather, it is Kabbalah as applied to the problems of the human psyche and of human life.

The *Tanya* is clearly a book about morals and morality, a guide for those trying to find a way to reach higher and to become more refined spiritual beings. It is a story of war, the eternal—or at least, the very consistent—battle raging within every human being. In this story, the person himself is not the actor; he is the battlefield.

In studying this struggle, it is of course important to identify the parties at war—what are these facets of man that are engaged in constant battle? Interestingly enough, the book of the *Tanya* defines the two sides not as good and evil, and also not as body vs. spirit. It is not, in essence, the children of darkness against the children of light, though at times it does come to that. Instead, it calls it a war of the animal against the Divine.

Man is basically a creature of zoology, but he is also created from a Divine mold. These two sides of humanity are clashing constantly over the question of identity: Who am I, and how can I be defined? *Tanya* seeks to clarify for its readers the distinction between the animal and Divine parts of man and to explain why they are in intrinsic—and unending—disagreement with one another.

In this book, the animal soul does not have the base definition that often comes to mind. The *Tanya* does not view the animal as the domain of the so-called carnal desires or physical needs. Rather, it speaks about the self—that level of man that views itself as the beginning of everything. No creature of zoology can really think about anything without using itself as a starting point: I exist, I am the center of everything, I am the purpose of everything, and from here I go on. The essence of man's purpose is this struggle to get out of the self, to break free of his animalistic confines in order to connect with the Divine.

While the description of this battle within each human being is an important part of the book, the *Tanya* also tries to devise strategies to help people win this war. It teaches how one can do better and how one can give the side of the "good" some ability to effectively overcome its opponent.

The study of *Tanya* is a demanding one, but it is perhaps one of the most approachable means to Kabbalah. Like many other pieces of Hasidic literature, the *Tanya* has taken some of the most grand and abstract notions of the world and put them in such a way that they become meaningful in life. In a very practical way, this book offers those seeking a more spiritual existence the formulas through which they can better know God, and better know themselves.

Reprinted with permission from Kosher Spirit Magazine, March 2006.

Ideas from this essay are expounded upon in Rabbi Steinsaltz's Learning From the Tanya: Volume Two in the Definitive Commentary on the Moral and Mystical Teachings of a Classic Work of Kabbalah (Jossey-Bass, 2005).

Getting in Touch with the Inner Ewe: Taming Your Wild Side

by **Rabbi Shais Taub**

There is a war going on. Neither side will settle for less than complete domination of our very lives.

The two camps are two forces within us; two souls that keep us alive.

The G-dly soul is selfless, peaceful and unwaveringly dedicated to the service of the Divine. This soul is enthralled by spiritual matters only and finds mundane pleasures repellent.

Then there's the animal soul: ego-driven, unsettled, given over to the pursuit of pleasure. He thrives on stimuli and seeks out all things physical. All notions of any "higher purpose" leave him terrifically bored. If we are to approach the Infinite, to cling to G-d, we must see to it that the G-dly soul forever dominates its animalistic counterpart.

This is the war. But after the smoke is clear, how shall we deal with the vanquished beast? To set him free would be dangerous. To eliminate him entirely may be imprudent. (After all, who'll remind us to eat lunch the next day?) Chasidic thought offers us an ideal game plan for dealing with the animal soul—an age-old dynamic mastered by zookeepers and farmers long ago. The animal soul left unchecked will disrupt, even oppose the attainment of spiritual goals. Could we expect any different?

But if we master the animal, put him under the yoke, and train him, at once his intensity and might become our own. We teach him to take pleasure in the Divine. Redirect his focus. Now he pulls the wagon and we ride.

This week's Torah portion, Vayikra, describes the Jew and his offering that he brings to G-d upon the altar of the Temple. The Torah tells us that the offering shall be from him, the Jew. The Chasidic masters teach that this is the animal each one of us must bring to G-d, the animal inside us whose sublimation is a most unique and pleasant offering to G-d.

Everyone's animal is different. Some of us have a rowdy ox. Others exhibit the distinct qualities of a stubborn goat. And some people have an indulgent little sheep inside. But these traits—all of the animal's special quirks—can become assets in serving G-d. When pointed in the right direction, our animals become the most energetic, staunch, and persistent workers in reaching spiritual goals.

And who knows? Once the animal gets going, he might even teach the mellow G-dly soul a thing or two.

Reprinted with permission from the author

Lesson **2**
Getting a Grip on Yourself

Introduction

Sometimes, life feels like one big masquerade party. Your inner child is dressed in high heels or a business suit, while your outer parent is busy throwing a major temper tantrum . . . It can be hard at times to tell what's really you and what's just there for show.

In this lesson, we take a close look at insides and outsides, and how to get the two halves to fit into a single whole.

Conflict
Review of Lesson 1

Table **1**

10 Faculties	**3** Garments
Insides	Outsides
What you want	What you do
Self	Self-Expression
Composition of Soul	Modes of Expression of Soul

Table 2

10 Faculties of Animal Soul

Insides

What you want

Self

Composition of Soul

10 Faculties of G-dly Soul

Insides

What you want

Self

Composition of Soul

3 Garments

Outsides

What you do

Self-Expression

Modes of Expression of Soul

Learning Exercise 1

Your instructor will assign the roles of animal soul and G-dly soul. You will need to respond to the following dilemma while keeping to your assigned role.

You asked your neighbor to lend you his hedge clippers last weekend. Although he wasn't using them, he refused to let you have them. This weekend, just as you finish using your leaf blower, he comes over and asks to borrow your leaf blower because his is broken.

The Small City

Text 1

כי הגוף נקרא עיר קטנה

וכמו ששני מלכים נלחמים על עיר אחת

שכל אחד רוצה לכבשה ולמלוך עליה . . .

כך שתי הנפשות האלקית והחיונית הבהמית

. . . נלחמות זו עם זו על הגוף וכל אבריו

שהאלקית חפצה ורצונה שתהא היא לבדה המושלת עליו ומנהיגתו . . .

אך נפש הבהמית . . . רצונה להפך ממש

The body is called a "small city" (Kohelet/ Ecclesiastes 9:14). Just as two kings wage war over a city which each wishes to capture and rule . . . so the two souls—the G-dly soul and the vitalizing animal soul . . . wage war against each other over the body and all its limbs. The G-dly soul's will and desire is that it alone rule and direct the person . . . and the animal soul desires the very opposite.

TANYA, CHAPTER 9

And the Winner is . . . : Two Extremes Cases
The *Tsadik*

Text 2 📜

הנה כשהאדם . . . (ו)נלחם כל כך עם הבהמית
עד שמגרש ומבער הרע שבה מחלל השמאלי . . . נקרא צדיק

When a person . . . wages war against the animal soul to the extent that he banishes and eradicates its evil from . . . [inside of himself] he is called . . . a *tsadik*.

TANYA, CHAPTER 10

Figure 1
The *Tsadik*

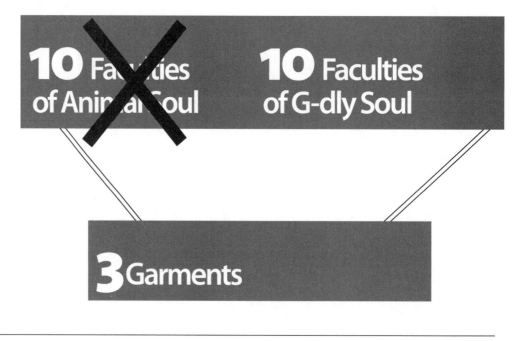

10 Faculties of Animal Soul   10 Faculties of G-dly Soul

3 Garments

Text 3

… (להתענג בם) דהיינו למאוס מאד בתענוגי עולם הזה
… מחמת גודל אהבתו לה'

A tsadik despises mere gratification of the physical appetite because of his great love of G-d [which is mutually exclusive with the pursuit of pleasure for its own sake].

TANYA, CHAPTER 10

The *Rasha*

Text 4

… וזה מתחלק … לרבבות מדרגות חלוקות
יש מי שהכפיפה והביטול אצלו מעט מזער
… ואף גם זאת אינו בתמידות
… אלא לעתים רחוקים מתגבר הרע על הטוב וכובש את העיר קטנה
… אך לא כולו אלא מקצתו לבד
דהיינו או במעשה לבד לעשות עבירות קלות ולא חמורות חס ושלום
או בדיבור לבד … או במחשבה לבד הרהורי עבירה
… ואחר כך גובר בו הטוב שבנפשו האלהית ומתחרט
ויש מי שהרע גובר בו יותר
ומתלבש' בו כל שלשה לבושים של הרע
… ומחטיאו בעבירות חמורות יותר ובעתים קרובים יותר אך בינתיים מתחרט
… אלא שאין לו התגברות כל כך לנצח את הרע לפרוש מחטאיו

The category [of *rasha*] is subdivided into myriads of degrees . . . . [On one end of the spectrum], there is one in whom only on infrequent occasions does the evil prevail over the good, conquering the "small city" . . . . And [even then] not all of the body falls under its dominion, but only part of it . . . . Namely, the animal soul prevails either in deed alone, in the commission of minor transgressions, not major ones, G-d forbid; or it may prevail in speech alone, or in thought alone, in contemplations of sin . . . . After which, the good that is in his G-dly soul asserts itself and he is filled with remorse over his transgression . . . .

[On the other end of the spectrum there is one] in whom the evil prevails more strongly, and all three garments of evil clothe themselves in him, causing him to commit more heinous sins, and [to sin] more frequently. Intermittently, he too experiences remorse . . . . However, the good within him does not exert itself sufficiently to prevent him from sinning . . . .

Tanya, Chapter 11

The *Beinoni*
Definition of a *Beinoni*

Text 5

והבינוני הוא שלעולם אין הרע גובר כל כך לכבוש את העיר קטנה
להתלבש בגוף להחטיאו דהיינו ששלשה לבושי נפש הבהמית
. . . אין גוברים בו על נפש האלהית להתלבש בגוף . . .
רק שלשה לבושי נפש האלהית הם לבדם מתלבשים בגוף

The *beinoni* is one in whom [the animal soul] never attains enough power to conquer the "small city," so as to clothe itself in the body and make it sin. That is to say, the three "garments" of the animal soul . . . do not prevail over the G-dly soul to the extent of clothing themselves in the body . . . . Only the three garments of the G-dly soul manifest themselves in the body.

TANYA, CHAPTER 12

Text 6

רק מפני שלא לו לבדו משפט המלוכה והממשלה בעיר
אינו יכול להוציא תאותו מכח אל הפועל להתלבש באברי הגוף . . .
כי המוח שליט על הלב . . .
שכך נוצר האדם בתולדתו שכל אדם יכול ברצונו שבמוחו
להתאפק ולמשול ברוח תאותו שבלבו
שלא למלאת משאלות לבו במעשה דבור ומחשבה . .
ואף על פי כן אינו נקרא צדיק כלל
מפני שיתרון הזה אשר לאור נפש האלקית . . . אינו אלא בשלשה לבושי . . .

Although . . . the G-dly soul [of the *beinoni*] . . . does not hold undisputed sovereignty over the "small city," [nevertheless,] the animal soul is unable to implement its desire by clothing itself in the limbs of the body . . . because the brain naturally rules over the heart . . . . For man was so created from birth, that every person may, with the power of the will in his brain, restrain himself and control the drive of his heart's lust, preventing his heart's desires from finding expression in deed, word or thought . . . . Still, he is not deemed a *tsadik* at all, for the G-dly soul's dominance . . . is limited to the three garments alone.

TANYA, CHAPTER 12

The Third Garment: Willful Thought vs. Impulsive Thought

Text 7

אלא הרהורי עבירה . . . יכולים לפעול לעלות למוחו

. . . אלא מיד בעלייתו לשם דוחהו בשתי ידים

ומסיח דעתו מיד שנזכר שהוא הרהור רע

ואינו מקבלו ברצון אפילו להרהר בו ברצון

וכל שכן להעלותו על הדעת לעשותו חס ושלום או אפילו לדבר בו

כי המהרהר ברצון נקרא רשע באותה שעה

והבינוני אינו רשע אפילו שעה אחת לעולם

mpulsive thoughts of sin can manage to rise to his mind. However he will not entertain them willingly . . . . No sooner does it arise than he thrusts it aside with both hands, and averts his mind from it, the instant he realizes that it is an evil thought. He will refuse to accept it willingly even as a subject for mere fantasy and will certainly not entertain the notion of acting on it, G-d forbid, or even speaking of it. One who willingly indulges in such thoughts is deemed a *rasha* at that moment, but the *beinoni* is not a *rasha* even for a single moment.

TANYA, CHAPTER 12

Learning Exercise 2

For the next sixty seconds, you will picture an image in your mind and repeat a phrase in your head. For the purpose of the experiment, any image or phrase could be randomly chosen, but, in keeping with the spirit of this course, we will choose something holy. For the next sixty seconds, starting when I say "go," picture a Torah scroll and repeat over and over in your mind, "It is a tree of life for those who hold fast to it." When any other thought rises to your mind, be it an image or words, simply push it away. As long as you do not begin to purposely entertain these thoughts, you're doing just fine.

Start now.

Between Man and Fellow

Text 8 📜

וכן בדברים שבין אדם לחבירו
מיד שעולה לו מהלב למוח איזו טינא ושנאה חס ושלום
או איזו קנאה או כעס או קפידא ודומיהן
אינו מקבלן כלל במוחו וברצונו
ואדרבה המוח שליט ומושל ברוח שבלבו לעשות ההפך ממש
להתנהג עם חבירו במדת חסד וחיבה יתרה מודעת לו
לסבול ממנו עד קצה האחרון ולא לכעוס חס ושלום
וגם שלא לשלם לו כפעלו חס ושלום

So too, in matters between man and his fellow, as soon as there rises from his heart to his mind any animosity or hatred, G-d forbid, or jealousy, anger or a grudge, and their like, he will bar them from his mind and will. On the contrary, his mind will prevail over and dominate the feelings of his heart to do the exact opposite, and [he will] conduct himself toward his fellow with kindness, displaying disproportionate love towards his fellow. Even when extremely pained, he will not be provoked into anger, G-d forbid, or take revenge, G-d forbid.

TANYA, CHAPTER 12

Being in a *Beinoni* State of Mind

Learning Exercise 3

Every one of us can choose to be in the state of being a *beinoni* at any time. But rather than talk about it, let's experience it for ourselves.

For the next sixty seconds, refrain from allowing your animal soul any garments: that means thought, speech and action. Sitting around idly and doing nothing doesn't work, because that also indulges the animal soul's penchant for laziness. Also, it would constitute the failure to perform the *mitzvah* of Torah study at a time when we are able to do so. So, here's what we'll do. For the next sixty seconds, we will say the *Shema* prayer.

Read the prayer and don't think about anything else. If you finish, start over again, and if stray thoughts pop up in your mind, consciously return your mind to the text you are trying to read.

Text 9

והנה מדת הבינוני היא מדת כל אדם
ואחריה כל אדם ימשוך שכל אדם יכול להיות בינוני בכל עת ובכל שעה
כי הבינוני אינו מואס ברע שזהו דבר המסור ללב
ולא כל העתים שוות
אלא סור מרע ועשה טוב דהיינו בפועל ממש במעשה דבור ומחשבה
שבהם הבחירה והיכולת והרשות נתונה לכל אדם
לעשות ולדבר ולחשוב גם מה שהוא נגד תאות לבו (והפכה ממש)

Now, the state of being a *beinoni* is attainable by every person, and each person should strive after it, for every person can, at any moment, be a *beinoni*, because a *beinoni* does not abhor evil. That is something that is subject to [the feelings of] the heart, and may vary from time to time. But a *beinoni* merely [adheres to the injunction] to "turn away from evil and do good (Tehilim/Psalms 37:27)," in actual practice—in deed, speech, and thought—and it is in these matters that everyone is given the choice, ability and freedom to act, speak, and think [as he chooses] even when it is diametrically opposed to the desire of his heart.

Tanya, Chapter 14

Review and Conclusion
Tsadik, Rasha or *Beinoni*?

Learning Exercise 4

An old lady was riding the bus, carrying her groceries and her life savings of twenty thousand dollars in cash in her purse to bring to the bank. When she got off at her stop, she was horrified to realize that she had remembered her groceries but left her purse on the bus. She immediately called the police who called the bus company to ask if anyone had found the purse. An hour later, a man showed up to the police station with the purse and all of the money. Needless to say, the old lady was relieved and thanked the man profusely. The local news heard about the story and wanted to interview the hero who returned the money.

"Were you tempted to keep it?" they asked.

"Yes," he answered, "The moment I found the money, the first thing that popped into my head was to pay off my car and take a trip to the Bahamas. I had to literally force myself to go down to the police station and turn it in."

Assuming that the man in this story is expressing his typical reaction to all moral dilemmas, is he a *tsadik, rasha* or *beinoni*?

Key Points

1. The three garments—thought, speech, and action—can only be controlled by one of the two souls at any given time, and the two souls vie for control like two kings over the same kingdom.

2. A *tsadik* is one whose G-dly soul is completely in control while the animal soul lies completely dormant.

3. A *rasha* is one whose animal soul at times finds expression in the soul's garments.

4. While the *beinoni's* internal struggle mirrors that of the *rasha*, the *beinoni* is identical to the *tsadik* in behavior.

5. We can choose our thoughts, speech and actions—the garments of our soul.

6. Thought, as a garment of the soul, does not include impulsive, tangential thoughts that "pop into" our minds and intrude against our will; rather, the garment of thought refers to thoughts upon which we consciously choose to focus.

7. Everyone has the potential to achieve the rank of *beinoni,* by actively choosing which soul—G-dly or animal—is allowed garments of expression.

Additional Readings

Bonaparte and the Chassid

From the writings and talks of the sixth Lubavitcher Rebbe, Rabbi Yosef Yitzchak of Lubavitch

Translation/Adaptation by **Rabbi Yanki Tauber**

The renowned chassid Rabbi Moshe Meisels of Vilna, youngest of Rabbi Schneur Zalman's disciples, once told Rabbi Eisel of Homel: "The *aleph* of Chassidism saved me from a certain death."

[In his Tanya, Rabbi Schneur Zalman of Liadi states: "By its very nature, the mind rules the heart." This axiom, known as the "*aleph* of Chassidism," is a cornerstone of the Chabad-Chassidic approach to life.]

Rabbi Moshe Meisels, an extremely learned man, was fluent in German, Russian, Polish and French. During Napoleon's war on Russia he served as a translator for the French High Command. Rabbi Schneur Zalman had charged him to associate with the French military officials, to attain a position in their service, and to convey all that he learned to the commanders of the Russian army.[1] Within a short while Rabbi Moshe had succeeded in gaining the favor of the chief commanders of Napoleon's army and was privy to their most secret plans.

It was he, Reb Moshe, who saved the Russian arms arsenal in Vilna from the fate which befell the arsenal in Schvintzian. He alerted the Russian commander in charge, and those who tried to blow up the arsenal were caught in the act.

"The High Command of the French army was meeting," related Reb Moshe, "and hotly debating the maneuvers and the arrangement of the flanks for the upcoming battle. The maps were spread on the floor, and the generals were examining the roads and trails, unable to reach a decision. Time was short. Tomorrow, or, at the very latest, the day after, the battle on the environs of Vilna must begin.

"They were still debating when the door flew open with a crash. The guard stationed inside the door was greatly alarmed and drew his revolver. So great was the commotion, that everyone thought that the enemy had burst in, in an attempt to capture the French Chief Command.

"But it was Napoleon himself who appeared in the doorway. The Emperor's face was dark with fury. He stormed into the room and raged: 'Has the battle been planned? Have the orders to form the flanks been issued?'

"'And who is this stranger?!' he continued, pointing to me. In a flash he was at my side. 'You are a spy for Russia!' he thundered, and placed his hand upon my chest to feel the pounding heart of a man exposed.

"At that moment, the *aleph* of Chassidism stood me by. My mind commanded my heart to beat not an increment faster. In an unwavering voice I said: 'The commanders of His Highness the Emperor have taken me as their interpreter, as I am knowledgeable in the languages crucial to the carrying out of their duties . . .'"

Biographical notes:

Rabbi Schneur Zalman of Liadi, also known as the "Alter Rebbe" and "The Rav," was born in Li'ozna, White Russia, on the 18th of Elul 5505 (1745). He became a disciple of Rabbi DovBer of Mezeritch (the second leader of the Chassidic movement) in 1764. In 1772 he established the "Chabad" branch of the Chassidism. For twenty years he worked on his *Tanya*, in which he outlined the Chabad philosophy and ethos. First published in 1797, the *Tanya* is regarded as the "bible" of Chabad Chassidism upon which hundreds of works and thousands of discourses by seven generations of Chabad rebbes and their disciples are based. Rabbi Schneur Zalman passed away on the 24th of Tevet, 5583 (December 1812) while fleeing Napoleon's armies.

Rabbi Moshe Meisels was originally a disciple of Rabbi Eliyahu, the Gaon of Vilna, and a member of the opposition to the Chassidic movement. He later became a devoted chassid of Rabbi Schneur Zalman of Liadi, and, after the latter's passing, of Rabbi DovBer of Lubavitch and of Rabbi Menachem Mendel of Lubavitch. Rabbi Moshe served as the leader of the Chassidic community in Vilna until 1816 when he made *aliyah* ("ascent") to the Holy Land and settled in Hebron, where he passed away in 1849.

1. Rabbi Schneur Zalman actively supported the Czar against Napoleon during the Napoleonic Wars, both on the celestial level, intervening on high for a Russian victory, and by down to earth methods such as the Chassidic spy of our story. Rabbi Schneur Zalman was of the opinion that while Napoleon's plans of "emancipating" the Jewish community may bring respite from the harsh Czarist decrees and improved material conditions, this is but the glittering veneer of forced assimilation and spiritual genocide. The Rebbe's contribution to Russia's victory was recognized by the Czar, who awarded Rabbi Schneur Zalman and his descendents the status of "An Honorable Citizen For All Generations." Five generations of Chabad Rebbes were to make use of this special standing in their work on behalf of the Jews of Russia.

Reprinted with permission from chabad.org

Benefit of the Doubt

by **Rabbi Yaakov Lieder**

With righteousness shall you judge your fellow (Leviticus 19:15).

There is an interesting Torah law that states that a judge who has witnessed a crime is disqualified from acting as a judge in that case. The reason being that a person who witnessed a crime with his own eyes will not be able to objectively examine the defense case. True justice can only be done when the benefit of the doubt can be properly examined.

In workshops I conduct for parents, children and spouses seeking a better relationship between them, we have found that the best way to resolve a conflict is to first try to reduce the intensity of the negative feelings the parties have for each other.

I found that the following written exercise can be of great assistance to some people:

1) Describe the negative feelings you have toward your child/parent/spouse.

2) On a scale of 1-100, rate how intense your negative feelings are.

3) If you were hired to serve as your child/parent/spouse's defense attorney in a court of law, how would you describe the reasons for his or her action?

4) On a scale of 1-100, how strongly do you believe your defense arguments to be true?

5) Rate how intense your negative feelings are now, on a scale of 1-100.

The change in the intensity of the feelings may differ from person to person and from situation to situation, but it is very likely that the figure in #5 will be significantly lower than the figure in #2. It is amazing how this simple mental exercise will reduce the intensity of emotions such as anger, hurt, shame, etc., and the pain associated with them.

There are other ways in which engaging our minds to describe to ourselves certain events and situations will drastically affect our feelings about them. For example, we can describe a child or parent's action by saying, "He stabbed me in the back," and feel a strong stabbing pain. We can reduce it by describing it as, "He *punched* me in the back." We can choose to stay there, or, if we want to reduce it further, we can describe it as, "He was not honest with me," and so on.

Why not take the wonderful tool called the brain that G-d has given us, and utilize it to work for us rather than against us? By giving our loved ones the benefit of the doubt and using different descriptions to describe a negative action, we may not change the other person; but it will definitely change our feelings and reduce our pain, thereby enabling us to handle the situation more effectively, and perhaps even find solutions to some of the problems.

Try it—you'll like it!

Reprinted with permission from chabad.org

Mind Over Heart?

by **Rabbi Tzvi Freeman**

Getting your mind to rule over your heart is a common theme in Jewish teachings. It's also horribly misunderstood.

Most people, when they hear about the mind ruling over the heart, imagine a cold, calculated and stuck-up neurotic. After all, the mind is all those things. Wouldn't we much rather live with the vivacious, freedom-loving heart?

So we have to explain that when the mind is ruling the heart, it does not mean that the mind is at the top of the chain of command. Nobody wants the mind in charge— you'd never get anything done. The mind may be great at solving puzzles, but it's an incompetent idiot when it comes to real life. Rather, the mind is meant to be but a conduit for the soul.

You see, the soul, being beyond the body, has a higher vision. It also has some great ideas to express. But the soul needs to get the body involved in that vision and those ideas. And it knows the only way that can happen is by inspiring the heart.

Problem is, the soul is just too big for that little heart to contain. So when the soul makes a direct-line connection to the heart, the heart is overwhelmed. Sure, it may catch fire and burn wild for a while. But then it's all over and forgotten.

That's where the mind fits in. The mind has to reach up to the soul and catch some of its higher vision. Then it chews on that vision until it becomes real enough that the heart, as well, can relate to it. That's the point we call *Da'at*. Roughly translated as "realization". The point of, "Yeah! It really *is* that way!" That's the point where the heart kicks in, with lasting inspiration. It's the mind that gets the heart to that place.

To make this more real: Let's say you're a musician. You know your inspiration doesn't come from the mind—it comes from somewhere beyond that. But a lot of the time, it doesn't come at all. Your mind has to open up, tune in to something beyond itself. Then the juices flow and you can play with your heart.

But, on the other hand, all the time you are playing, you have to keep that mind in gear. If it slides out of the clutch and the heart takes over alone, the depth of the music is lost. Like jazz musicians say, you have to stay cool. That's what we call "mind over heart."

Okay, let's say you're not a musician. But maybe you like playing football. The same dynamics apply: If your heart is not into it, it just ain't gonna work. But if you let your heart go wild, you're not going to be in the league for too long.

So some people lose the mind and get caught up in the heart. Others forget about the heart and become wrapped up in the mind. Neither way is good. The point is to get the soul to express itself in the heart by reaching through the mind.

Getting this mind-heart thing down is not easy. First of all, during your initial exposure to life—known as childhood—you are basically an emotional animal, with little chance that the mind will have control of anything. Secondly, even once you grow up, the whole world is out to make you "just react" to their stimuli. After all, as long as you have control over your own brain and heart, it's kind of hard to sell you stuff you don't need and get you to work all those extra hours to pay for it. Most of the world feels much better if you leave them the keys to your brain and heart and just take a quiet place in the back seat, thank you.

So reclaiming your brain and heart for yourself is an upstream battle. *Tefillin* is one of those mitzvahs that provides a major boost to your forces. Take a few moments in the midst of the morning rush to put on *tefillin* and say the *Shema*. Then, during your day, remind yourself about who's in charge. That you don't have to give in to every whim of the heart. That you're higher than that. That you have a mind and a soul—all your own.

Reprinted with permission from chabad.org

Lesson 3
Sync or Sink

Introduction

Would you like to be a perfect person in just 30 days? Are you looking for a pill to solve your problems? Or have you made peace with the fact that meaningful change is a process which requires lots of patience, hard work, and dedication?

Whatever your preference, we've got something for you in this lesson. *Tanya* presents two methods—the "quick fix," for instant inspiration,and the long-term solution, for radical, fundamental change. Both are important—and we'll find out when each method is most useful, as well as the advantages and disadvantages of each.

The Long Way

Creating New Feelings

Learning Exercise 1

Imagine that one day you get a call, telling you that an aunt whom you haven't seen since you were a very young child is coming to stay for a week. It is hard to get excited about hosting someone you know so little about. So you call your mother who tells you that this aunt was her favorite sister growing up, and your mother tells you all sorts of stories about what this aunt meant to her, and how this aunt cared for you when you were young. Your mom even has some pictures of this aunt playing with you in the park, which she sends to you. Now those warm childhood memories start to flood your memory.

How does thinking about your aunt change your feelings about hosting her for a week?

Can you think of other situations in which you develop feelings and enthusiasm for a daunting task through contemplation and thinking?

Text 1

וזה כלל גדול בעבודת ה' לבינונים . . .
למשול ולשלוט על הטבע שבחלל השמאלי . . .
כשמתבונן במוחו בגדולת אין סוף ברוך הוא
להוליד מבינתו רוח דעת ויראת ה' במוחו
להיות סור מרע . . . ואהבת ה' בלבו . . .
לדבקה בו בקיום המצות דאורייתא ודרבנן

The important principle regarding the divine service of the *beinoni* . . . is to govern and rule the [animal] nature . . . . by intellectually contemplating the greatness of the Infinite, so as to create through understanding a spirit of knowledge and awe of G-d in his mind, which will cause him to turn away from evil . . . . And a love of G-d in his heart . . . [will cause him] to cleave to Him by fulfilling the precepts of the Torah.

TANYA, CHAPTER 16

וזה כלל גדול
בעבודת ה' לבינונים

Passion vs. Appreciation

Text 2

ויתר על כן צריך לידע כלל גדול בעבודה לבינונים

שגם אם אין יד שכלו ורוח בינתו משגת להוליד אהבת ה׳ בהתגלות לבו . . .

דהיינו שהלב מבין . . . גדולת א״ס ב״ה . . .

אשר על כן יאתה לו יתב׳ שתכלה אליו נפש כל חי

לידבק ולהכלל באורו . . .

ואי לזאת יאתה להן לחבקו בכל לב ונפש ומאד

דהיינו קיום התרי״ג מצות במעשה ובדבור ובמחשבה

שהיא השגת וידיעת התורה

Furthermore, one must know an additional important principle in the *beinoni's* service of G-d . . . . Even if one's intellect and understanding are incapable of producing a revealed love of G-d in his heart . . . [as long as he] comprehends . . . the greatness of the Infinite [this is completely acceptable]. For it is this appreciation that leads him to engage in the Torah and *mitzvot*.

TANYA, CHAPTER 16

Text 3

ודבר זה קרוב מאד ונקל לכל אדם אשר יש לו מוח בקדקדו
כי מוחו ברשותו ויכול להתבונן בו בכל אשר יחפוץ
וכשיתבונן בו בגדולת א״ס ב״ה
ממילא יוליד במוחו על כל פנים
האהבה לה׳ לדבקה בו בקיום מצותיו ותורתו . . .

To arouse a love which remains hidden in the heart is very easy and very near to every person who has a brain, for his mind is under his control even if his heart is not, and he can meditate with it as he pleases, on any subject. Thus, if he uses it to contemplate the greatness of the Almighty, he will inevitably generate—in his mind, at least—a love of G-d, and cleave to Him through the performance of His commandments and the study of His Torah.

TANYA, CHAPTER 17

The Short Way
The Hidden Love

Text 4

אַף מִי שֶׁדַּעְתּוֹ קְצָרָה בִּידִיעַת ה׳
וְאֵין לוֹ לֵב לְהָבִין בִּגְדוּלַת אֵ״ס בָּ״ה
לְהוֹלִיד מִמֶּנָּה דְּחִילוּ וּרְחִימוּ אֲפִילוּ בְּמוֹחוֹ וּתְבוּנָתוֹ לְבַד
אַף עַל פִּי כֵן קָרוֹב אֵלָיו הַדָּבָר מְאֹד לִשְׁמוֹר וְלַעֲשׂוֹת
כָּל מִצְוֹת הַתּוֹרָה וְתַלְמוּד תּוֹרָה . . .
בִּדְחִילוּ וּרְחִימוּ שֶׁהִיא אַהֲבָה מְסוּתֶּרֶת שֶׁבְּלֵב כְּלָלוּת יִשְׂרָאֵל
שֶׁהִיא יְרוּשָׁה לָנוּ מֵאֲבוֹתֵינוּ

Even for the person who has only a limited understanding of G-d's greatness, and does not have sufficient emotional capacity to generate through contemplation an understanding of the awe and love he should feel for G-d, it is still a "very near thing" for him to guard and to practice all the commandments of the Torah as well as the study of Torah . . . [by accessing] the hidden love already present in the heart of all Jews bequeathed to us from our patriarchs.

TANYA, CHAPTER 18

Text 5

ולכן אפילו קל שבקלים ופושעי ישראל
מוסרים נפשם על קדושת ה׳ על הרוב וסובלים עינוים קשים
שלא לכפור בה׳ אחד ואף אם הם בורים ועמי הארץ
ואין יודעים גדולת ה׳ . . .
ואין מוסרי׳ נפשם מחמת דעת והתבוננות בה׳ כלל
אלא . . . בלי שום טעם וטענה ומענה כלל

Therefore, generally speaking, even the most careless sinners among Israel sacrifice their lives for the sanctity of G-d's name and suffer harsh torture rather than deny G-d's unity, even if they are unlearned and ignorant of G-d's greatness . . . . Their self-sacrifice does not result from any knowledge or contemplation of G-d but rather . . . without any reason or rational argument whatsoever.

TANYA, CHAPTER 18

The Power of a *Mitzvah*

Text 6 📜

שני דברות הראשונים אנכי ולא יהיה לך הם כללות כל התורה כולה
כי דבור אנכי כולל כל רמ״ח מצות עשה
ולא יהיה לך כולל כל שס״ה מצות לא תעשה . . .

The first two commandments in the Decalogue: "I am the L-rd [your G-d] . . ." and "You shall have no other gods," comprise the entire Torah. The commandment: "I am G-d" contains all the 248 positive precepts, while the commandment: "You shall have no other gods" contains all the 365 prohibitive commandments.

TANYA, CHAPTER 20

Text 7 📜

שכמו שהיה הוא לבדו הוא יחיד ומיוחד קודם הבראם
כן הוא לבדו הוא יחיד ומיוחד אחר שבראם
משום דכולא קמיה כלא חשיב וכאין ואפס ממש

Just as G-d was One alone, single and unique, before [the worlds] were created, so is He One alone, single and unique after He created them, because all is as naught beside Him, as if absolutely nonexistent.

TANYA, CHAPTER 20

Text 8

ואין שום שינוי כלל לפניו יתברך

אלא אל הברואים המקבלים חיותם מבחינת דבורו יתברך

. . . ע״י השתלשלו׳ מעלה לעלול וירידת המדרגו׳ בצמצומים רבים ושונים

עד שיוכלו הברואים לקבל חיותם והתהוותם ממנו

. . . ולא יתבטלו במציאות

. . . אך לגבי הקב״ה אין שום צמצום והסתר והעלם מסתיר ומעלים לפניו

משום שאין הצמצומים והלבושי׳ דבר נפרד ממנו ית׳ ח״ו

אלא כהדין קמצא דלבושי׳ מיניה וביה

For G-d, nothing whatever was changed [by having created. The change] exists only from the perspective of the created beings, who receive their life-force from Him . . . by means of numerous and various contractions, so that the created beings can derive their life-force and existence without losing their identity . . . . Yet, in regard to G-d, no concealment or veil hides or obscures anything from Him . . . for the contractions and the veils are not things distinct from Him, Heaven forfend, but are rather "like the turtle whose garment [i.e., his shell] is part of its own body. (Midrash, Bereishit Rabah 21)"

TANYA, CHAPTER 21

Text 9

וְהַטּוּמְאָה אֵינָהּ בְּטֵלָה כְּלָל לְגַבֵּי קְדוּשַׁת הַקָּבָּ״ה . . .
וְלָכֵן אָמְרוּ רַזַ״ל שֶׁגַּסּוּת הָרוּחַ שְׁקוּלָה כַּעֲבוֹדָה זָרָה מַמָּשׁ
כִּי עִיקָר וְשׁוֹרֶשׁ עֲבוֹדָה זָרָה
הוּא מַה שֶּׁנֶּחְשָׁב לְדָבָר בִּפְנֵי עַצְמוֹ נִפְרָד מִקְּדוּשָׁתוֹ שֶׁל מָקוֹם . . .
וַהֲרֵי זוֹ כְּפִירָה בְּאַחְדוּתוֹ הָאֲמִיתִית

nholiness does not surrender itself at all to the holiness of G-d .... That is why the sages said that arrogance is truly tantamount to idolatry, for the essence and root of idolatry is the notion that something can be an entity independent and separate from the holiness of G-d. Thus, idolatry does not [necessarily] imply an outright denial of G-d .... but rather a denial of G-d's true Oneness [i.e., that there is nothing separate from Him].

TANYA, CHAPTER 22

Text 10

לְפִי שֶׁהַמִּצְוֹת הֵן פְּנִימִיּוּת רָצוֹן הָעֶלְיוֹן וְחֶפְצוֹ הָאֲמִיתִי (הַמְלוּבָּשׁ בְּכָל הָעוֹלָמוֹת)
כָּל חִיּוּתָם וְשִׁפְעָם תָּלוּי בְּמַעֲשֵׂה הַמִּצְוֹת
. . . עַל כֵּן גַּם אֵבְרֵי גּוּף הָאָדָם הַמְקַיְּימִים הַמִּצְוָה . . .
. . . הֵם נַעֲשׂוּ מֶרְכָּבָה מַמָּשׁ לִרְצוֹן הָעֶלְיוֹן . . .

he *mitzvot* constitute G-d's innermost will and His true desire .... The very life and sustenance of all the worlds is contingent upon the performance of the *mitzvot*. In this way, the limbs of

the human body that perform a *mitzvah* . . . become an
actual vehicle for the divine will.

Tanya, Chapter 23

Text 11

וזה לעומת זה הן שס"ה מצות לא תעשה דאורייתא וכל איסורי דרבנן

מאחר שהן נגד רצונו וחכמתו ית' והפכם ממש

הם נפרדים מיחודו ואחדותו ית' בתכלית הפירוד ממש . . .

וכן ג' לבושי הנפש שמקליפת נוגה שבישראל . . .

המלובשים בשס"ה לא תעשה דאורייתא ודרבנן

וכן מהות הנפש עצמה המלובשת בלבושיה

כולם מיוחדים ממש בסטרא אחרא וקליפה זו (הנקרה ע"ז) . . .

The exact opposite is so regarding the 365 prohibitions stated in the Torah and all of the rab-
binical prohibitions. Since they are contrary to
G-d's will and wisdom, they represent total and complete separation from His unity and oneness . . . . So,
too, the three garments of a Jew's [animal] soul . . . that
are invested in the 365 Torah-prohibitions or any of the
rabbinic injunctions, as well as the [animal] soul itself
which is clothed in its garments—they all become completely united with the unholiness of idolatry.

Tanya, Chapter 24

Text 12 📖

אבל באמת לאמיתו
אפילו עבירה קלה הרי העוברה עובר על רצון העליון ב״ה
והוא בתכלית הפירוד מיחודו ואחדותו ית׳ . . .

I n truth, even he who commits a minor sin transgresses the divine will and is completely separated from G-d's unity and oneness . . . . at the time he commits [the transgression].

TANYA, CHAPTER 24

Triggering the Instinct

Text 13 📖

שבכל עת ובכל שעה בידו של אדם וברשותו הוא
להעביר רוח שטות והשכחה מקרבו
ולזכור ולעורר אהבתו לה׳ אחד המסותרת בודאי בלבבו בלי שום ספק
וזה שכתוב ״ובלבבך״ ונכלל בה גם דחילו
דהיינו שלא ליפרד בשום אופן מיחודו ואחדותו יתברך
אפילו במסירת נפש ממש בלי שום טעם ושכל מושג
אלא בטבע אלהי וכל שכן בשבירת התאוות הקלה מיסורי מיתה . . .
. . . אפילו מעבירה קלה של דברי סופרים . . . מאחר שנפרד בה מיחודו
ואחדותו כמו בעבודה זה ממש בשעת מעשה

A t any time and moment a person can arouse his love of the one G-d that is undoubtedly latent in his heart. This is the meaning of "[It is near to you] in your heart (Devarim/Deuteronomy 30:14)." This love also contains an aspect of fear; that is, the dread of being separated from G-d's unity and oneness even if it means sacrificing his life without any reason or logic, but purely out of one's G-dly nature. Surely, it is far easier to subdue one's appetites [than to endure] the suffering of death , yet he would readily do that if need be.

He will thus be moved to obey G-d's will . . . . even when it concerns a minor rabbinic prohibition . . . since at the time that he does the forbidden act, he becomes separated from G-d's unity just as much as through actual idolatry.

TANYA, CHAPTER 25

Text 14

והן בבחינת ועשה טוב להתגבר כארי בגבורה ואומץ הלב
נגד היצר המכביד את גופו ומפיל עליו עצלה
שלעמוד נגדו ולכבשו קרוב מאד אל האדם . . .
קל מאד מיסורי מיתה ה' ישמרנו . . . שלא ליפרד מיחודו ואחדותו יתברך
אפילו לפי שעה להשתחות לעבודה זרה חס ושלום
וכל שכן שיש לו לקבל באהבה וברצון
כדי לדבקה בו לעולם ועד

Likewise in the category of "doing good"—[he will be able] to strengthen himself like a lion with might and determination of heart against the evil nature which weighs down his body . . . . It is very easy for a person to resist and subjugate his nature when he considers that doing so is much less painful than enduring the pangs of death—May G-d preserve us! Yet he would lovingly and willingly have accepted the pain of death (May G-d preserve us!) so as not to be separated from G-d's unity and oneness even for a moment by an act of idolatry, G-d forbid. Certainly, then, he ought to lovingly and willingly accept [any inconvenience or burden] in order to bind himself to G-d with an eternal bond.

TANYA, CHAPTER 25

Learning Exercise 2

We started the lesson by talking about changes that you have made in your life. Some were probably made the "long way." These are changes that took you a long time to make, but that are likely to be lasting, because they came about as a result of reflection. An example of this might be the decision to give up smoking.

You make other changes the "short way." They come about because your latent instinctive feelings of fear, or love, etc. are aroused by a certain stimulus. For example, you might hear about a terrible car accident in which someone flew through the windshield. The next day, you buckle up your seat belt. Unfortunately, the change is not likely to last very long.

Think of a change you have made in your life. Discuss with a classmate: Was the impetus for this change more like the long way or more like the short way?

Why?

Appendix
Additional Texts

Text A

With this, we will understand the verse: "For this matter is very near to you, in your mouth and in your heart, that you may do it (Devarim 30:14)." At first glance, the statement that it is "very near to your heart" seems contrary to our experience . . . for it is not a "very near thing" to change one's heart from worldly desires to a sincere love of G-d . . . . Moreover, our Sages have said that only *tsadikim* have control over their hearts. However, the [later] clause "that you may do it" [qualifies that this] refers merely to a love which is sufficient to lead to the fulfillment of the commandments.

TANYA, CHAPTER 17

Text B

This love [of G-d] found in the G-dly soul . . . is called "hidden love," for it is hidden and veiled in the case of the transgressors . . . for whom a "spirit of foolishness" leads them to sin . . . . However, when they are confronted with a test of faith . . . . [the foolish spirit is dispelled and they] withstand the test of self-sacrifice.

TANYA, CHAPTER 19

Key Points

1. Impulse control alone is very difficult when our impulses are not consonant with our actions, so we need to work on ways to build emotional congruity. There are two methods for doing so, which are best used in combination: the "long way" and the "short way."

2. The "long way" consists of comprehensive study or contemplation—creating feelings through knowledge. It takes a lot of time to take effect, but its effects are lasting.

3. The "short way" involves tapping into our latent, natural feelings of love and yearning for G-d. These feelings of love and yearning for G-d come to the fore when our connection with G-d is under threat. Therefore, one can arouse these feelings by viewing each *mitzvah* as an opportunity to connect with G-d, and by viewing any transgression as, G-d forbid, threatening that connection with G-d.

4. The advantage of the "short way," as compared with the "long way," is its quick results, though its effects can also wane with similar speed.

Additional Readings

Jewish Meditation

by **Rabbi Nissan Dovid Dubov**

The Talmud tells the story of a thief who prayed to G-d for success. Is this thief a believer or not? If yes, what is he doing thieving? If not, then why pray to G-d? The answer is that he does believe, only his belief is peripheral and he has not internalized his faith to the extent that it has had an effect on his entire way of thinking, feeling, and behaving. Belief must be intellectualized, internalized, and integrated into one's actions, and that is the purpose of Jewish meditation.

Sadly, most Jews today have never heard of Jewish meditation, and typically, when asking a group of Jews how many of them meditate on a regular basis, the answer is only a few.

Many people associate meditation with eastern religion but few associate it with a regular synagogue service. The truth is, however, that meditation is an essential ingredient of our religion and the base of all observance. There are 613 *Mitzvot* in the Torah. Six of them are obligatory every single second of the day, and upon deeper reflection we see they are the bedrock of observance. They are:

1. To believe in G-d.

2. To unify His name.

3. To love G-d.

4. To fear Him.

5. To love a fellow Jew.

6. Not to turn astray after one's heart and eyes.

The first step is to believe in and to know G-d, as the verse states, "Know this day and take unto your heart that the L-rd is G-d; in the heavens above and upon the earth below there is nothing else," (Deuteronomy 4:39). We proclaim His unity by reciting, "Hear O Israel, the L-rd our G-d, the L-rd is One," twice a day, morning and evening. Such profound statements of belief cannot simply be recited by rote; rather they must be accompanied by deep contemplation. To do them justice a person must enter a course of study where one will learn such concepts as the nature of G-d, the chain order of creation, and the purpose of this creation, and then deeply meditate upon what has been learned. The point of the meditation is to arouse the emotions of love and fear of G-d, which allows one to grasp the profundity of such statements as those cited above.

The *Zohar* calls love and fear the two wings with which the bird soars above. A person is motivated to keep all the positive commandments out of a sense of love and commitment, and one is deterred from transgressing the negative commandments out of a sense of fear. There are, of course, many levels of love and fear (also expressed as awe) as explained at length in *chassidic* teachings. The scriptural text uses the Hebrew word *Yirah*, usually translated as the "fear" of G-d. However, fear denotes fear of punishment, which is the most basic level of fear. In truth, the more appropriate translation is "awe," for that denotes deep awareness of the Omnipotent Being. Initially, a person may be deterred from sin by a fear of punishment, however ultimately the deterrent should be a deep sense of awe and desire not to contradict the Divine will.

The Maggid of Mezritch once asked, "How is it possible for G-d to command an emotion?" The Torah states that we are to "Love the L-rd your G-d," and to "Love your fellow Jew as yourself." Love is a very powerful emotion and very personal. How can G-d demand that all His creatures love Him and each other? Is it possible to switch on an emotion impulsively upon demand? The Maggid answers that the command is not to instantly become emotional, rather the command is to meditate.

Deep meditation and intimate knowledge of G-d brings one to love Him, and contemplation on the G-dly essence of every individual leads one to love every Jew.

By extension, a person's love and fear of G-d is reflected in their inter-human relationships and in their steadfast commitment to not stray after the heart and eyes, as the Baal Shem Tov stated, "The portal to G-d is the love of a fellow Jew." When applying this idea to the daily prayers, we see that if prayer is to be effective during the course of the day, it must involve meditation. Although classically prayer is a request to G-d, on a deeper level, prayer constitutes two soul movements—the moment when one meditates on deeply attaching the soul to G-d, while simultaneously, communicating with one's *Nefesh HaBehamit* in an effort to refine one's character.

When the Sages constructed the order of prayer, they did so with this in mind, and each stage of the prayers is a rung in the ladder of meditation. We begin with *Modeh Ani*, which is a simple expression of faith. We then express our deep thanks to G-d for our faculties and well-being in the morning blessings.

We proceed to the section describing the daily sacrifices, which is called in Hebrew *korbanot*. The word *"korban"* actually means to "draw near." Spiritually this means that we all need to sacrifice our animalistic nature on the altar of the heart.

Through fiery and passionate love of G-d, we can burn excess and indulgence and draw near to true service. Next, we read the *Pesukei D'Zimrah* (verses of praise), where we become truly overwhelmed by G-d's benevolence and omnipotence. We then speak of the service of the angels and how they stand in awe in their daily lauding of G-d. Following this we proclaim G-d's absolute unity in the *Shema*, realizing that G-d is all and all is G-d. Only then do we stand for the *Amidah* and request from G-d.

This daily service cannot be rushed or done without preparation, and it must be realized that the order and words are precise and meaningful. It also requires a solid comprehension of its meaning, both literally and conceptually. But beyond that, it requires personalization. We should reflect on what it means to us individually, how it will help us change for the better, and how it has

an impact on daily life. Meditation gives us the tools not only to understand the words of the prayers, but to carry these words and their meaning into our daily lives when we engage in the day-to-day activities that can sometimes seem far from obvious G-dliness. This is why *chassidim* of *ChaBaD* placed such emphasis on the study of *chassidic* teachings before prayer. It gives the mind and heart focus and language with which to meditate and integrate.

Most important is the discipline of training oneself that a rich spiritual experience cannot be gained by rote, rather by exertion of the mind and body focusing and internalizing.

Meditation requires practice and study. For the beginner, a good place to start would be to decide that before one prays one should sit quietly for a few moments and "know before whom you stand." One should study a particular discourse in Chassidism that explains in detail the dynamics of G-d's unity, or the love and fear of Him, and one should reflect regularly on that discourse. Most important is that this meditation be of a detailed nature and not just cursory reflection. The more detailed the meditation, the stronger its effect.

Reprinted with permission from chabad.org

Active vs. Passive Meditation:

Active meditation emanates G-dliness; passivity only reinforces the ego.

by Rabbi **Schneur Zalman Stern**

Hitbonenut is the Jewish mystical discipline of *active* thought-meditation. In 1986 a collection of Hebrew manuscripts, roughly 200 years old, written by Rabbi Schneur Zalman of Liadi (the first Lubavitcher Rebbe), was published. One of these manuscripts (*Ma'amorim Ketzarim, Inyonim*, p. 133) discusses passive versus active thought-meditation. This amazingly contemporary treatise sheds light on some of the pitfalls of passive meditation, and lends insight into the distinctions between passive and active meditation. The following is a translation and adaptation of this manuscript into English, followed by a few notes.

There are two different methods of thought-meditation:

1) The *first method* entails centering and settling one's consciousness on the general sense of an idea, while passively withdrawing from all thoughts, feelings, and body sensations.

The one who meditates disengages and contracts the mind, and in no way increases the breadth or detail of understanding. This is done by fixating on a point of awareness in an uninterrupted stream of consciousness for approximately half an hour, which brings the person to the general state of "airy vision". (This may take weeks or months of preparation to accomplish).

Airy vision results from thought-meditation that uses the superficial powers of the intellect to divest the idea that is the focus of the meditation of any concrete definition. By thus abstracting the idea, the person will come to perceive through the mind's eye the subtle spirit of the idea as an airy vision devoid of tangible meaning. In this context the prophets said, "And they will be swept away by the [cosmic] wind," and "When you will gaze upon [the idea] it will be naught." As a result of this type of meditation, many people have been misled and deluded by their own imagination and by charlatans who promote futile and vain visions for their own gain.

Little deliberation is required to recognize this type of meditation. A few simple indications may be: a) As bodily tensions are released, the person may experience slight twitching, jerking or nervous movements. b) As the emotions are settled and calmed, a slight turbulence, disturbance or racing may be felt in the heart. c) The mind is empty of thoughts, and all thoughts that arise dissipate. d) There is an increase in self-awareness.

2) The *second method* demands detailed, broad, and deep comprehension, as opposed to withdrawing from the intellect. This process requires intense mental exertion to increase one's awareness of the open, simple, and revealed meaning of the idea, to scrutinize and elaborate on the concept's many details, facets and ramifications, and not to allow the mind to contract and settle on one point alone. The indications for the second type of meditation are profoundly different than the indications for the first type.

There is no passive dissipation of the energies of the body, heart, and mind whatsoever; rather, there is active exertion, concentration, and channeling of all the person's powers into the mind. This intense mental exertion is so all-consuming that the person has no sensation of "self" at all.

The awareness achieved through active thought-meditation is very different from the consciousness reached through passive meditation, where the person is susceptible to imaginings, vain visions and futile delusions. To the contrary, the person enclothes the idea in many metaphors and analogies until it is thoroughly comprehended and the truth can be perceived vividly through the mind's eye.

Another indication that one is engaged in active thought-meditation is the yearning to grasp new insights into the idea; to discover in every nuance the implicit and specific meaning. The person will be entirely oblivious to the "self," for the mind's total preoccupation with the idea completely overshadows any sensations of the heart.

Regarding the ecstasy and awakening that come through the first type of meditation, the person will find the arousal exceedingly euphoric. This happens because the meditative process of emptying one's mind is specifically directed toward bringing exhilaration into the "self". In actuality, this state constitutes a dualism between G-d and the individual. The person inescapably becomes egoistic and is ultimately distant from and in direct opposition to G-dliness; he returns strongly to his sense of "self" being connected [or worse, "soars upward like an eagle and proclaims 'I am and there is no other.'"].

In contrast, with the second type of meditation, enlightenment comes only through channeling and emanating G-dliness (as a by-product). The person is not preparing the "self" to experience a revelation, but rather, is absorbed in intense mental exertion and is devoted to the vivification of a Torah insight. Enlightenment is spontaneously triggered by the Torah's G-dly wisdom, through "gazing at the Glory of the King and nothing else," and not because the person has cleared the mind *in order* to receive a revelation.

Nor is the person enthralled by accompanying feelings of ecstasy, for the conscious awareness of "self" has no prominence at all, making exhilaration and other associated sensations irrelevant. So it is written, "The fool does not desire [true] enlightenment," but seeks feelings of ecstasy. Moreover, the fool's perpetuation of self-centeredness shuts out even the faintest glimmer of G-dly enlightenment.

Another distinction is that the ecstasy experienced through the first type of meditation may cause a person to feel high and mighty, and to become callous, overbearing and flippant. He will likely acquire a heightened sensitivity to and an increased appetite for sensual pleasures. Through the second method, however, the person becomes truly humble and no longer esteems the "self" to be central. He is also far from desiring transient pleasures and relating to contemptible character traits, like indignation, oppressiveness, frivolity, etc. Such a person regards any negative characteristics he finds within himself as repulsive and deplorable, takes no credit for personal accomplishments, and considers the "self" to be veritably nothing at all.

COMMENTS:

[Gleaned from Rabbi Hillel Paritcher's commentaries on *Shaar HaYichud* and *Kuntres HaHispaalus*, written by Rabbi Dov Ber, the second Rebbe of Lubavitch]

Lack of self-centeredness does not imply sublimation, denial or loss of individuality. To the contrary, centering upon G-dliness liberates the spirit, whereas holding on to one's awareness of "self" obstructs spontaneity, creativity and enthusiasm. As an unsought and automatic result of attaining G-dly enlightenment, one may be imbued with Supernal Delight, the highest form of human pleasure. Yet the person is not carried away by this elation and does not give in to it. His intention remains purely to offer delight to G-d through his alignment with the Supreme Will.

To gain a clearer understanding of how to practice *Hitbonenut*, active thought-meditation, much more explanation is needed. For example, it is taught that one should not meditate exclusively on a single isolated metaphor, but rather on the complete world-view which results from the synthesis of many metaphors. To do this, the one meditating must dwell at length on the precise meaning of several ideas until the kernel of each idea crystallizes in his understanding. Then he should broaden the viewpoint until the ideas can be seen through the mind's eye in a single glance, as one unified insight. By gazing with the mind's eye deep into this unified insight, the first level of enlightenment may be realized, which is the enthusiasm of the natural soul (the astral body). Next, if he will go beyond the limits of the physical body and natural soul, through purity of intention and increased intensity in the meditation, the second level of enlightenment may be attained, namely the awakening of the G-dly attributes of the higher soul. On the third level, the G-dly attributes of the higher soul illuminate and permeate the attributes of the natural soul, which are based in the power centers of the physical body — action, emotion, thought, will, and pleasure.

Reprinted with permission from kabbalaonline.org

Lesson 4
The Joyride

שִׂמְחָה

Introduction

Is your glass half-empty or half-full? The answer lies in the perspective you choose to take. Because happiness is an action, not a reaction; it is state of mind, not a state of being; it lies not in your position but in your disposition.

In this lesson, you will learn how to keep life from getting you down, and the secret to greeting each day with genuine joy and optimism.

Troubleshooting
The Tactical Importance of Joy

Text 1

ברם כגון דא צריך לאודעי כלל גדול
כי כמו שנצחון לנצח דבר גשמי
כגון שני אנשים המתאבקים זה עם זה להפיל זה את זה.
הנה אם האחד הוא בעצלות וכבדות ינוצח בקל
ויפול גם אם הוא גבור יותר מחבירו
ככה ממש בנצחון היצר אי אפשר לנצחו בעצלות וכבדות
כי אם בזריזות הנמשכת משמחה . . .
ופתיחת הלב וטהרתו מכל נדנוד דאגה ועצב בעולם.

But this is a cardinal principle, that with a victory over a physical opponent—for instance, two people who wrestle each other, each striving to fell the other—if one of them is lazy and sluggish he will easily be defeated and will fall, even if he is stronger than the other. Similarly with the conquest of one's evil nature; it is impossible to conquer it with laziness and sluggishness . . . but rather with exuberance which derives from joy, and an open heart that is unblemished by any trace of worry and sadness in the world.

TANYA, CHAPTER 26

Dealing with Life's Problems

Text 2

והנה עצה היעוצה לטהר לבו
מכל עצב ונדנוד דאגה ממילי דעלמא ואפילו בני חיי ומזוני
מודעת זאת לכל מאמר רז"ל כשם שמברך על הטובה כו'
ופירשו בגמרא לקבולי בשמחה
כמו שמחת הטובה הנגלית ונראית
כי גם זו לטובה רק שאינה נגלית ונראית לעיני בשר
שהוא ו"ה משם הוי"ה ב"ה כי היא מעלמא דאתכסיא שלמעלה מעלמא דאתגלייא
ועלמא דאתכסיא הוא י"ה
וז"ש אשרי הגבר אשר תיסרנו י"ה וגו'

Sound advice has been offered by our sages on cleansing one's heart of all sadness and of any trace of worry about worldly matters, even children, health, or livelihood . . . .

The Talmud explains that one should accept [misfortune] with joy, just like the joy in a visible and obvious good. For this, too, is for the good, except that it is not apparent and visible to mortal eyes, for it stems from the "hidden world," which is higher than the "revealed world."

TANYA, CHAPTER 26

Guilt Must Be Carefully Controlled

Figure 1

Guilt → Indulgence → Degradation → Guilt (cycle repeats)

Text 3 📖

אך העצבות ממילי דשמיא צריך לשית עצות בנפשו לפטר ממנה

אין צריך לומר בשעת עבודה שצריך לעבוד ה׳ בשמחה ובטוב לבב

אלא אפילו מי שהוא בעל עסקים ודרך ארץ

אם נופל לו עצב ודאגה ממילי דשמיא בשעת עסקיו

בידוע שהוא תחבולת היצר כדי להפילו אחר כך בתאוות ח״ו כנודע

שאם לא כן מאין באה לו עצבות אמיתית

מחמת אהבת ה׳ או יראתו באמצע עסקיו

As for sadness connected with spiritual matters, one must seek ways and means of freeing oneself from it. That this applies to the time of prayer is obvious, for] one must pray to G-d with joy and gladness of heart. But even if one is occupied in business and worldly affairs, if there should descend upon him any sadness or anxiety about spiritual matters during his business affairs, it is certainly a trick of the Evil Inclination in order to lure him afterwards into lusts, G-d forbid, as is well known. For if it were not so, whence would a genuine sadness, one that is derived from love or fear of G-d, come to him in the midst of his business affairs?

TANYA, CHAPTER 26

Text 4 🦋

והנה בין שנפלה לו העצבות בשעת עבודה בתלמוד תורה או בתפלה
ובין שנפלה לו שלא בשעת עבודה
זאת ישים אל לבו כי אין הזמן גרמא כעת לעצבות אמיתית
אפילו לדאגת עונות חמורים ח"ו.
רק לזאת צריך קביעות עתים ושעת הכושר
בישוב הדעת להתבונן בגדולת ה' אשר חטא לו
כדי שעל ידי זה יהיה לבו נשבר באמת במרירות אמיתית

Whether this depression [caused by feelings of guilt over his past] settles upon him during his service of G-d in Torah study or prayer, or when he is occupied with other things, this is what he should consider: Now is not the proper time for genuine sadness or worry even over grave sins, G-d forbid. For that, one must set aside opportune times, when the mind is calm, to reflect on the greatness of G-d against Whom he has sinned, so that thereby his heart will truly be rent with genuine bitterness.

TANYA, CHAPTER 26

The Futility of Shame

Text 5

וְאִם הָעַצְבוּת אֵינָהּ מִדַּאֲגַת עֲוֹנוֹת

אֶלָּא מֵהִרְהוּרִים רָעִים וְתַאֲווֹת רָעוֹת שֶׁנּוֹפְלוֹת בְּמַחֲשַׁבְתּוֹ . . .

אַדְּרַבָּה יֵשׁ לוֹ לִשְׂמוֹחַ בְּחֶלְקוֹ שֶׁאַף שֶׁנּוֹפְלוֹת לוֹ בְּמַחֲשַׁבְתּוֹ

הוּא מֵסִיחַ דַּעְתּוֹ מֵהֶן לְקַיֵּים מַה שֶּׁנֶּאֱמַר וְלֹא תָתוּרוּ אַחֲרֵי לְבַבְכֶם

וְאַחֲרֵי עֵינֵיכֶם אֲשֶׁר אַתֶּם זוֹנִים אַחֲרֵיהֶם.

וְאֵין הַכָּתוּב מְדַבֵּר בְּצַדִּיקִי׳ לְקָרְאָם זוֹנִים ח״ו אֶלָּא בְּבֵינוֹנִים כַּיּוֹצֵא בּוֹ

שֶׁנּוֹפְלִים לוֹ הִרְהוּרֵי נִיאוּף בְּמַחֲשַׁבְתּוֹ בֵּין בְּהֶיתֵּר כו׳

וּכְשֶׁמֵּסִיחַ דַּעְתּוֹ מְקַיֵּים לָאו זֶה

. . . וְעַל כֵּן צָרִיךְ לִשְׂמוֹחַ בְּקִיּוּם הַלָּאו כְּמוֹ בְּקִיּוּם מִצְוַת עֲשֵׂה מַמָּשׁ

f, however, his sadness does not stem from anxiety over sins that he has committed, but from the fact that sinful thoughts and desires enter his mind, then . . . on the contrary, he should be happy with his lot. For although these sinful impulses enter his mind, he averts his attention from them and thereby fulfills the injunction, "You shall not follow after your heart and after your eyes, by which you go astray (Bamidbar/Numbers 15:39)." The above verse surely does not speak of *tsadikim*, referring to them as "going astray," (G-d forbid) but of *beinonim* like himself in whose mind there do enter erotic thoughts whether of an innocent nature [or otherwise], and when he averts his mind from them, he fulfills this commandment . . . . Consequently, he should rejoice at his compliance with the injunction just as he does when performing an actual positive precept.

TANYA, CHAPTER 27

Text 6

ואדרבה העצבות היא מגסות הרוח שאינו מכיר מקומו
ועל כן ירע לבבו על שאינו במדרגת צדיק
שלצדיקים בודאי אין נופלים להם ההרהורי שטות כאלו
כי אילו היה מכיר מקומו שהוא רחוק מאד ממדרגת צדיק
והלוואי היה בינוני ולא רשע כל ימיו אפילו שעה אחת
הרי זאת היא מדת הבינונים ועבודתם
לכבוש היצר וההרהור העולה מהלב למוח . . . כנ״ל

On the contrary, such sadness is due to conceit. For he does not know his place and that is why he is distressed—because he [is upset that] he has not attained the level of a *tsadik* to whom such foolish thoughts do not occur. If he knew his place [he would see] that he is very far from the rank of *tsadik*, and that his greatest aspiration should be to become a *beinoni* and not a *rasha* for even a single moment throughout his life. [He would also understand] that [grappling with his impulses] is an appropriate task for *beinonim* and [it is in fact] their very mission in life—to subdue the evil impulse and the thought that rises from the heart to the mind . . . as explained above.

Tanya, Chapter 27

Learning Activity 1

Consider the following two scenarios. The first is an example of guilt as a result of having engaged in an unwanted action.

The second is an example of shame, as a result of realizing that you possess unseemly urges.

1. I made a commitment to have a Shabbat dinner every Friday night with my family. Last week, things were hectic at the office and I couldn't make it. I've been feeling guilty about it all week.

2. I am ashamed to admit it, but even when I have kept my commitment in the past, I find myself envying my friends who go out on Friday nights. I often daydream right in the middle of the meal that I could be out on the town with my friends, having all sorts of fun.

Suggest an appropriate way to deal with the feelings of guilt in the first case, and an appropriate way to deal with the feelings of shame in the second case.

Identifying with the Soul

Learning Activity 2

Make a list of those things that you want out of life. Be honest and don't censor yourself. You may write that you want to finish school or that you want to lose twenty pounds. Maybe you want to learn how to pray in Hebrew, to dance at your children's weddings, or to retire early and travel the world. Write your dreams, aspirations and goals.

Text 7

וזאת תהיה עבודתו כל ימיו בשמחה רבה

היא שמחת הנפש בצאתה מהגוף המתועב

ושבה אל בית אביה כנעוריה בשעת התורה והעבודה . . .

ואין לך שמחה גדולה כצאת מהגלות והשביה

כמשל בן מלך שהיה בשביה וטוחן בבית האסורים ומנוול באשפה

ויצא לחפשי אל בית אביו המלך

ואף שהגוף עומד בשיקוצו ותיעובו . . .

כי מהותה ועצמותה של הנפש הבהמית לא נהפך לטוב

. . . מכל מקום תיקר נפשו בעיניו לשמוח בשמחתה יותר מהגוף הנבזה

שלא לערבב ולבלבל שמחת הנפש בעצבון הגוף

This, then, should be one's lifelong [aim]—the joy of the soul upon leaving the body during one's study of the Torah and prayer [so that the soul may] return to "her father's house as in her youth" . . . . [Surely,] there is no joy as great as that of being released from exile and captivity. It is comparable to the joy of a prince who was taken captive, turning the millstone in prison and becoming covered with filth, who then goes free to the house of his father, the king. True, the body remains [a source of limitation] . . . since the essential character of the animal soul has not been transformed to good. But his G-dly soul will become more precious to him than his body, so that he rejoices in the soul's joy without letting the sadness on account of his body interfere with or disturb the joy of the soul.

TANYA, CHAPTER 31

Love Your Fellow as Yourself

Text 8 🕯

והנה על ידי קיום הדברים הנ״ל
להיות גופו נבזה ונמאס בעיניו רק שמחתו תהיה שמחת הנפש לבדה
הרי זו דרך ישרה וקלה לבא לידי קיום מצות ואהבת לרעך כמוך
לכל נפש מישראל למגדול ועד קטן.
כי מאחר שגופו נמאס ומתועב אצלו
והנפש והרוח מי יודע גדולתן ומעלתן בשרשן ומקורן באלקים חיים.
בשגם שכולן מתאימות ואב אחד לכולנה
ולכן נקראו כל ישראל אחים . . . רק שהגופים מחולקים.
ולכן העושים גופם עיקר ונפשם טפלה
אי אפשר להיות אהבה ואחוה אמיתית ביניהם
אלא התלויה בדבר לבדה

Acting on the advice mentioned above—to view one's body with scorn and contempt, and to find joy in the joy of the soul alone—is a direct and easy path toward fulfilling the *mitzvah*, "You shall love your fellow as yourself (Vayikra/Leviticus 19:18)," with regard to every Jew both great and small. For his body is despised, while who can know the greatness of the soul and spirit in their source and root—the living G-d? Furthermore, they are actually all equal; they all have one Father. Therefore, all of Israel are [each] literally called "brothers." Only their bodies are distinct from each other. Therefore, there can be no true love and fraternity between those who regard their bodies as primary and their souls as secondary, but only [a love] that is conditional.

TANYA, CHAPTER 32

Rejoicing in the Nearness of G-d

Personal Joy

Text 9

עוֹד זֹאת תִּהְיֶה שִׂמְחַת הַנֶּפֶשׁ הָאֲמִיתִית

וּבִפְרָט כְּשֶׁרוֹאֶה בְּנַפְשׁוֹ בְּעִתִּים מְזוּמָּנִים

שֶׁצָּרִיךְ לְזַכְּכָהּ וּלְהָאִירָהּ בְּשִׂמְחַת לֵב

אֲזַי יַעֲמִיק מַחֲשַׁבְתּוֹ וִיצַיֵּיר בְּשִׂכְלוֹ וּבִינָתוֹ עִנְיָן יְחוּדוֹ יִתְ׳ הָאֲמִיתִי

אֵיךְ הוּא מְמַלֵּא כָּל עָלְמִין עֶלְיוֹנִים וְתַחְתּוֹנִים

וַאֲפִילוּ מְלֹא כָל הָאָרֶץ הַלֵּזוּ הוּא כְּבוֹדוֹ יִתְ׳ וְכוּלָּא קַמֵּיהּ כְּלָא חֲשִׁיב מַמָּשׁ

וְהוּא לְבַדּוֹ הוּא בָּעֶלְיוֹנִים וְתַחְתּוֹנִים מַמָּשׁ

כְּמוֹ שֶׁהָיָה לְבַדּוֹ קוֹדֶם שֵׁשֶׁת יְמֵי בְרֵאשִׁית

וְגַם בִּמְקוֹם הַזֶּה שֶׁנִּבְרָא בּוֹ עוֹלָם הַזֶּה הַשָּׁמַיִם וְהָאָרֶץ וְכָל צְבָאָם

הָיָה הוּא לְבַדּוֹ מְמַלֵּא הַמָּקוֹם הַזֶּה

וְגַם עַתָּה כֵּן הוּא לְבַדּוֹ בְּלִי שׁוּם שִׁינּוּי כְּלָל

מִפְּנֵי שֶׁכָּל הַנִּבְרָאִים בְּטֵלִים אֶצְלוֹ (בִּמְצִיאוּת) . . .

Yet another means of leading one's soul to true joy, especially at those specific times when one finds it necessary to purify his soul and illuminate it with a gladness of heart is this: Let him then think deeply and picture in his mind the idea of G-d's true unity. Let him consider how He permeates all worlds, both upper and lower. Let him consider how even this world is filled with His glory and how everything is of no reality whatsoever in His presence. He is One alone in the upper and lower realms, just as He was One alone prior to the six days of Creation. Even in the very place where this world—the heaven, the earth and all their legions—was created, He alone then filled this space.

And the same is true now; He is One alone, without any change whatsoever. For in relation to Him, the very existence of all created beings is utterly nullified. When one will deeply contemplate this, his heart will be gladdened and his soul will rejoice . . . in this faith which [allows him to feel] the nearness of G-d, which is [after all] the whole [purpose] of man and the purpose of his creation and the creation of the . . . worlds: That He may have this abode here below.

TANYA, CHAPTER 33

Double Joy

Text 10

והיא שמחה כפולה ומכופלת
כי מלבד שמחת הנפש המשכלת בקרבת ה' ודירתו אתו עמו.
עוד זאת ישמח בכפליים
בשמחת ה' וגודל נחת רוח לפניו ית' באמונה זו
(דאתכפיא סטרא אחרא ממש)
ואתהפך חשוכא לנהורא . . . שבעולם הזה החומרי . . .
ואין שמחה לפניו ית' כאורה ושמחה כיתרון אור הבא מן החשך דייקא.
וז"ש ישמח ישראל בעושיו
פירוש שכל מי שהוא מזרע ישראל יש לו לשמוח בשמחת ה'
אשר שש ושמח בדירתו בתחתונים

This is a double and redoubled joy. Apart from the soul's joy upon apprehending how near G-d is to him and how He dwells together with him, he will also rejoice doubly in the joy and pleasure which his faith brings to G-d, whereby . . . the darkness . . . of this corporeal world is changed to light . . . for there is no joy before [G-d] like the light and joy of the unique quality of light that emerges from darkness. This is the meaning of the verse, "Let Israel rejoice in his Maker (Tehilim/Psalms 149:2)," that is to say, that every descendent of Israel should rejoice in the joy that G-d feels in dwelling here below.

TANYA, CHAPTER 33

Joy at Being G-d's "Host"

Text 11

זאת ישיב אל לבו כי מהיות קטן שכלי ושרש נשמתי מהכיל
להיות מרכבה ומשכן ליחודו ית׳ באמת לאמיתו
מאחר דלית מחשבה דילי תפיסא ומשגת בו ית׳ כלל וכלל שום השגה בעולם
ולא שמץ מנהו מהשגת האבו׳ והנביאים
אי לזאת אעשה לו משכן ומכון לשבתו הוא העסק בתלמוד תורה
כפי הפנאי שלי בקביעות עתים ביום ובלילה
כדת הניתנה לכל אחד ואחד בהלכות תלמוד תורה
וכמאמר רז״ל אפילו פרק אחד שחרית כו׳
ובזה ישמח לבו ויגיל ויתן הודאה על חלקו בשמחה ובטוב לבב
על שזכה להיות אושפזיכן לגבורה . . .

e should reflect in his heart as follows: "The capacity of my intelligence and of my soul's root is too limited to constitute a chariot and an abode for G-d's unity in perfect truth, for my

mind cannot grasp or apprehend His unity at all with any degree of comprehension in the world; not one iota, in fact, of that which was grasped by the patriarchs and prophets. This being so, I will make Him a sanctuary and an abode by studying Torah at fixed times by day and by night, to the extent of my free time, as stipulated by the law governing each individual's situation, set forth in the Laws of Torah Study. As our sages say, 'Even one chapter in the morning and one at night (Menachot 99b).'" Thereby, his heart shall rejoice; he shall be glad and offer praise and thanks for his fortune with a joyous and happy heart, that he has merited to act as G-d's host .... And even the remainder of the day, when he is engaged in commerce, he will provide a dwelling for Him [in his business affairs] by giving charity.

TANYA, CHAPTER 34

ובזה ישמח לבו

Key Points

1. The process of self-change can be both difficult and daunting, and without an attitude of joy and optimism, one may lose the motivation and edge one needs to continue.

2. One can feel hopeful in the face of life's challenges by reflection on the fact that everything that G-d does is good—though good can sometimes manifest itself in a concealed manner, rather than a revealed manner.

3. One can resolve feelings of guilt by appointing particular times to review past actions and develop a concrete plan for improvement, but unchanneled feelings of guilt are non-productive and cannot be allowed to weigh down the entire day.

4. Shame is utterly futile. Instead of feeling depression because of the ongoing struggle with temptation, one should view it as an opportunity: through overcoming the challenge, one is serving G-d.

5. A shift in self-concept, so that one identifies primarily with the soul rather than the body, is the key to experiencing the joy that results whenever we do a *mitzvah*.

6. When we view our fellow Jews primarily as souls and not bodies, we are able to genuinely love them as ourselves, and sense that, truly, we are all one.

7. Engaging in *mitzvot* allows us to fulfill our life purpose of building a "dwelling for G-d in the lower realms." It is a source of great joy that we are able to live purposefully and feel close to Him.

8. There is added joy in our feeling of "privilege" in being G-d's partner and host in this world.

Additional Readings

Music Is Playing

by **Devorah Leah Mishulovin**

The music is blasting—the walls are vibrating and my little daughter is dancing. He walks into the room, looks at the little one, turns to me, and asks, "Why is she dancing?"

"The music is playing," I inform him.

He is deaf.

He doesn't hear the music. But he trusts me as his friend. And now he comprehends why my little one is moving her body and jumping. There is sudden reason to her strange movements. Our young friend's visit to our home last week was a real eye-opener for me; it made me realize that there is depth and breadth beyond what we experience.

Our friend was not born deaf and is therefore, thank G-d, able to talk. It was our responsibility to make ourselves "heard," according to the language he comprehends. Between his lip reading, good old-fashioned writing messages with pen and paper, finger spelling and the modern technology of texting, we managed. But it was an experience very different from what we are used to. I am grateful to my family for their persistence and ingenuity in finding ways to communicate.

Can you imagine not being able to hear? Not the bird's chirp or the car's honk, the pitter-patter of the raindrops, or the baby crying? To sit at a table full of people and not hear the conversation? Think about having no use for your phone (besides texting). Think about not hearing *kiddush, havdalah*, the Torah reading. Think about how isolating that can be.

I drove him to a coffee shop and waited outside. He came right back out, coffee-less, saying they were out of coffee. "Then can you ask them where the closest coffee place is?" I tell him. "I can't hear them," he replies simply

with a shrug. Oh. I forgot. So we went in together and he settled for an iced cappuccino.

You'd think he would be sad or frustrated, right? Not our young man. He takes everything in stride, is chirpy, loves to talk and has a great sense of humor. He is intelligent, very independent and, generally, a happy person. He roughhoused with the kids, built a house out of blocks, and read them stories. His "difficulties" were not a hindrance to living, to thriving.

At the bookstore, he shows me a book he wants to buy—stories about overcoming life struggles. I mouth to him that he can write his own book.

Watching him navigate the course of his life made me realize that I, too, am deaf: a different kind of deaf. Actually, we all are, to a certain degree. I am deaf to G-d's "strange movements." Strange to me, that is. His actions puzzle me. I look at Him in wonderment. "G-d, what are you doing? Why is this one so ill? Why am I so poor? Why was she born retarded? Why did you take my father so young? Why did you make me so weak? Why did he miss his plane? Why were they in an accident?" And so on.

"There is music playing," I am told.

I am deaf. I don't hear the music. But I trust Him. There is reason, there is purpose. I don't need to know what the music is and I don't need to hear the lyrics. Music is defined as *"any sweet, pleasing, or harmonious sounds or sound."* That is enough for me. The music is blasting. G-d is "dancing." Unfortunately though, most of us, most of the time, are deaf. We cannot hear it. Nonetheless, it's comforting for me to know that there *is* music.

This past week we practiced patience and sensitivity. We learned that there are many ways to communicate. Our friend showed us that being joyful does not depend on outside elements. We saw how one can transform a limitation into a lesson, make lemonade if G-d gives you lemons, and enjoy every sip.

The main eye opener for me was just that—to have my eyes opened and see how real deafness is experienced. To live with this for a week and internalize the lessons. When I experience hardships or difficulties, I should not allow it to destroy me and pull me down. I have to remember there is a purpose in them, and that should give me the strength to overcome obstacles and continue to live, to thrive, and to flourish—joyfully.

My world may be "vibrating." I must trust, though, that there is good reason for it. May the day come, very soon, when I *will* hear the sweet, pleasant harmonious sounds *with* the lyrics, too, and comprehend the reasoning behind our challenges. For now though—it's enough for me to know that there *is* music playing.

Reprinted with permission from chabad.org

The Chassidic Approach To Joy

Understanding: The Core Of Joy
by **Rabbi Shloma Majeski**

Simchah, joy, is one of the most essential elements of the *Chassidic* way of life. Indeed, in the early stages of the *Chassidic* movement, before the name *chassidim* was coined, one of the temporary names used to refer to *chassidim* was *di freilicha,* meaning, "the happy ones." How could you define and identify a *chassid*? By seeing if he was *b'simchah*—happy and joyous.

The Rebbeim, the leaders of the *Chassidic* movement, would always emphasize the importance of happiness and would urge their followers to strive to eradicate all traces of sadness and depression. R. Shlomo of Karlin would say that depression is considered the threshold of all evil. On another occasion, R. Shlomo said that although the 365 negative commandments do not include a commandment not to be depressed, the damage that sadness and depression can cause is worse than the damage that any sin can cause.

The Baal Shem Tov [1] would say that there are times, when the *yetzer hora* (the evil inclination) tries to persuade a person to commit a sin, that it does not care whether or not the person will actually sin. What it wants is that after sinning, the person will become depressed and overcome with sadness. In other words, the depression that follows the sin can cause more spiritual damage than the actual sin itself.

The *Chassidic* emphasis on joy has its roots in the teachings of the *Kabbalah.* In that vein, the *AriZal* (see glossary) notes that the Torah [2] tells us that several harsh punishments will come "because you did not serve G-d with happiness and a glad heart." Other commentaries [3] explain that the intent of the verse is that the punishments will come because the people did not serve G-d in a time of pleasantness and joy. The *AriZal* explains [4], however, that the verse should be understood simply. What is the reason for the punishments that will befall our people? Their Divine service lacked *simchah*; they lacked the vitality, energy, and connection to G-d that joy contributes to Divine service.

When a person is depressed or sad, his energy is drained; he becomes weak and it is possible that his evil inclination will overpower him. By analogy: If two people are wrestling each other, and one of them is stronger, he will be able to overpower the weaker one. If, however, the stronger person is depressed and lacks vitality, and the weaker person is full of energy, the weaker person will be able to overcome the stronger person [5].

To refer back to the analogy: When a person is happy and full of energy, he can overcome his evil inclination. But even if he is spiritually strong, when a person is sad and his energy is drained, his *yetzer hora* can easily overcome him.

One might ask: Why are such teachings identified with *Chassidic* thought? Seemingly, these concepts would be accepted by people from all sectors of Jewish thought. Indeed, if they were extended slightly, they could be understood and accepted by secular thinkers as well. So why are they identified with *Chassidism*?

The answer [6] is that the theoretical basis that enables a person to translate these ideals from the abstract into the actual is inherent to *Chassidism*. *Chassidism* teaches that the vitality, and indeed the entire existence, of the world depends totally upon G-d. Every element of creation is one with G-d. Without this Divine energy, nothing could exist.

This leads to the appreciation of *hashgachah pratis*, Divine Providence. Everything that transpires, not only what happens to people, but also everything that happens to inanimate objects, comes as a direct result of G-d's will. Not only does every entity in the world exist by virtue of G-d's life-force; every event that occurs in the world takes place because G-d causes it to happen [7].

The awareness of these concepts leads directly to *simchah*. For a person who is aware that everything that happens to him is controlled by G-d will surely be happy. Indeed, when a person lacks such happiness, he is implying, Heaven forbid, that what is happening is *not* connected to G-d, or that G-d is causing it to happen, but that, Heaven forbid, G-d is not good.

This is a direct denial of G-d. If one believes that G-d is responsible for everything that happens, and believes that G-d is good, then naturally everything that happens is good.

If a person got up and made a declaration that everything that happens does not come from G-d, he would be denying G-d's oneness. Even when one refrains from making such statements, but acts in a way that implies so—for example, if he is sad—the implication is the same.

Indeed, actions speak louder than words. So by being sad, a person is denying the oneness of G-d. He is denying the fact that everything in the world is constantly connected to G-d, and everything that happens is controlled by Divine Providence.

This is why *Chassidism*, which stresses so clearly and so powerfully the connection between the creation and G-d, places such an emphasis on *simchah*. In addition to the contribution of *simchah* to our Divine service—for as above, when a person is sad, he becomes weak and vulnerable, and his evil inclination can overpower him—something far larger than one's individual self is involved. Happiness and its opposite depend on whether or not one is aware of G-d's oneness and His constant providence.

In this context, we can understand a unique concept taught by our Sages. Our Sages state [8] that a person who loses his temper is considered as if he worshipped idols. What is the connection between losing one's temper and idol worship?

Losing one's temper is obviously undesirable. It reflects a lack of self-control; it is socially unacceptable; but how is it connected to idol worship? The answer is that when a person loses his temper, he, in essence, is denying that what has occurred is coming from G-d. If he believed that everything that happens comes from G-d, that G-d is good and whatever G-d does is good, there is no room for losing one's temper, just as there is no room for depression and sadness.

A person once came to R. Dov Ber, the Maggid of Mezeritch, and asked him, "Rebbe, our Sages tell us that we must bless G-d when something good happens, and in the same way, we should bless G-d when something negative happens [9]. How can this be actualized?"

The Maggid of Mezeritch told him, "Go to my student, R. Zushya. He will explain it to you."

When he found R. Zushya, by looking at his face and his clothing he could easily see that he had not had much to eat, and that he did not have the money to buy decent clothing. Everything about him bespoke privation, but his face radiated happiness. "This is surely a person who can answer my question," he said to himself.

So he told R. Zushya that the Maggid had sent him to him to explain how a person could bless G-d in the face of adversity.

R. Zushya looked at him in puzzlement. "I do not know how to answer this question," he replied. "This question should be answered by someone who has suffered. I have never experienced suffering in my life."

R. Zushya was telling him that everything that happens comes from G-d and is controlled by Divine Providence.

He knew clearly that G-d is completely good. Therefore, it was as clear as day to him that everything that happens is good. And so, R. Zushya never experienced any suffering in his life.

Notes:

1. *Tzavos HaRivosh,* ch. 44.

2. Deuteronomy 28:47.

3. *Rashi, loc. cit.*

4. *See Likkutei Sichos,* Vol. XX, p. 552.

5. *See Tanya,* Chapter 26.

6. *See Tanya, Iggeres HaKodesh*, Epistle 11.

7. *See* the essay entitled *Master Plan: The Baal Shem Tov's Unique Conception of Divine Providence* (*Sichos In English*, 5752).

8. *Zohar,* Vol. I, p. 27b, *Mishneh Torah, Hilchos De'os* 2:3; *cf. Nedarim* 22b. See also *Tanya, Iggeres HaKodesh*, Epistle 25.

9. *Berachos* 54a.

The Key to Happiness

Excerpt from *Toward a Meaningful Life—The Wisdom of the Rebbe* by **Rabbi Simon Jacobson** (William Morrow & Company, 1995)

Man can never be happy if he does not nourish his soul as he does his body.
—The Rebbe

What is your life like?

If you are like most people, it is made up of countless bits and pieces of fragmented activity: exercise, work, eating, conversations, entertainment, sleep. Add up the pieces day after day, year after year, and you end up with an entire life split into millions of fragments, with no connecting thread. Fragmentation rattles our peace of mind, creating untold tension and anxiety. Over time, the fragments pile up and begin to suffocate your soul, the inner you that craves focus, purpose, and direction. Is it any wonder that after forty or fifty years of slogging through such disjointed days we wake up and suddenly wonder, "Is this what life is about? Am I really happy?"

A happy life is synonymous with a meaningful life, and we all want to live meaningful lives. We constantly strive to make our mark on humanity, to contribute something worthwhile to our world.

By acknowledging that within your body is a G-dly soul, a soul that can give your life purpose and lift it above the mundane pursuits of everyday life, you begin to put the pieces of your fragmented life in order. You see your life from a larger perspective, sanctifying every moment of your life—not only while you are studying or praying or doing charitable deeds, but while you are eating and sleeping, at home or at work, while traveling or on vacation. Instead of carrying out your daily activities by rote, you discover the G-dliness within each of them.

The Key to Happiness: Uniting Body and Soul

To be a happy, wholesome, and healthy person, your body and soul must work in perfect harmony. This means uniting the body and soul to fulfill the mission for which we were all put on earth: to lead a meaningful, productive, and virtuous life by making this physical world a home for G-d.

The body and soul, however, are in constant conflict: the body basically looking to satisfy its needs with the soul looking for transcendence and unity. The first step in dealing with this conflict is to acknowledge that the struggle exists, and be aware of the two distinct forces. Thinking that we are a single entity leads to confusion and despair: One day we are virtuous and the next we are selfish; one day we are motivated, the next we procrastinate.

The only way to unite body and soul is to accept that G-d is far higher than our limited selves. The soul, because of its transcendent nature, can rise above selfishness more easily than the body, and can discipline the body, through study and prayer, to recognize its true mission. Only then can the body rise to its true prominence—when it serves as a vehicle for the soul instead of acting under its own power, with its selfish wants and needs. Once the body recognizes the soul's dominance and makes peace with its twin sister, the tension can be properly harnessed.

Happiness Requires Action

It is not enough to acknowledge your soul; you must actualize it by partnering it with the body to help a neighbor in need, to listen to a friend in distress, to help provide food or clothing to someone who cannot afford it. These become more than simple good deeds; they become vital nourishment for your soul and a means of putting your physical body to good spiritual use.

True happiness is the fusion of body and soul dedicated to a higher cause, a cause that benefits humankind and gives meaning and inner peace to the individual in the process.

Action

When you awake in the morning, while you are still lying in bed, think for a moment: What does it mean to be awake and alive? Begin each day with a prayer; thank G-d for the new day. Acknowledge your soul. Think about what you would like to accomplish that would make today a meaningful day. If you train yourself to do this every morning, you will immediately begin to see your life in a new, sharper focus.

You should end your day just as you begin it. As you prepare for sleep, review the day and how you used its opportunities. Recognize that G-d has put you here for a purpose, and that all your activities should express that purpose. Go to sleep with the resolve that no matter how good—or bad—today was, tomorrow will be better. By doing so, your sleep will be more peaceful, and your waking more meaningful.

"Every person has both a body and a soul," said the Rebbe. "It is like a bird and its wings. Imagine if a bird were unaware that its wings enabled it to fly, they would only add an extra burden of weight. But once it flaps its wings, it lifts itself skyward. We all have wings—our soul—that can lift us as high as we need to go. All we have to do is learn to use them."

Pursuing Happiness

Savor the moment, take control of your time, and more secrets of the happiest people

by **Dr. David G. Myers**

During its first century, psychology focused far more on negative emotions such as depression, anger, and anxiety than on positive emotions such as happiness and satisfaction. Even today, our texts say more about suffering than about joy.

That is now changing. A new cadre of researchers is offering a fresh perspective on an old puzzle: Who are the happy people? Does happiness favor those of a particular age, sex, or race? Does wealth enhance well-being? Does happiness come with having certain traits? A particular job? Close friends? An active faith?

In 1993, I reported on what I found to be the four important traits of happy people: self-esteem, optimism, extroversion, and personal control. As an update, I offer the following material—gleaned from studies of several hundred thousand people in 16 countries—which hopefully offer further insight into happiness and what you can do to achieve it.

To begin with, if I wanted to predict whether you feel happy and find life satisfying, there are some things that, surprisingly, it would not help me to know. For example:

Tell me your age, and you've given me no clue. We can forget tales of "midlife crisis," "empty-nest syndrome," and despondent old age. Actually, happiness is equally available to people at every age. Moreover, rates of depression, suicide, and divorce show no increase during the mythical midlife crisis years.

Tell me your sex, and you've given me no clue. The sexes are prone to different sorts of misery. When troubled, men more often become alcoholic, while women more often ruminate and get depressed. Yet men and women are equally likely to declare themselves "very happy" and "satisfied" with life.

Tell me your race, and you've given me no clue. African-Americans, for example, are only slightly less likely than European-Americans to feel very happy. Yet how could this be, given what everyone knows—that disadvantaged groups suffer impoverished self-esteem and resulting depression? It's because what "everyone knows" is wrong.

Social psychologists Jennifer Crocker and Brenda Major explain: "A host of studies conclude that blacks have levels of self-esteem equal to or higher than that of whites." The National Institute of Mental Health's study of *Psychiatric Disorders in America* similarly revealed that rates of depression and alcoholism among blacks and whites are roughly equal.

Tell me your income, and—assuming you can afford life's necessities—I'm still in the dark as to whether you're a happy person. Most people suppose otherwise. They are not crass enough to say that money buys happiness. But they do think that 20 percent more money would make them a little happier. And three in four students—nearly double the proportion in 1970—now begin college agreeing that it's "very important" that they become "very well off financially."

Again, the findings astonish us: People in rich countries are not consistently happier than people in not-so-rich countries. (During the 1980s, the West Germans had double the incomes of the poorer Irish, who year after year reported more satisfaction with their lives,) And rich people—even those surveyed among *Forbes'* 100 wealthiest Americans—are only slightly happier than working-class folk.

So what would give us a clue about someone's level of happiness and how can we use this information to improve our inner well-being? Although there is no surefire "How to Be Happy" formula, here are a few suggestions:

Realize that enduring happiness doesn't come from "making it." What do you long for? Fame? Fortune? Unlimited leisure? Imagine that I could snap my fingers and give it to you. Would you now be happy? Indeed, you'd be euphoric, in the short run. But gradually you would adapt to your new circumstance and life would return to its normal mix of emotions. To recover the joy, you would now need an even higher high.

The consistent finding from dozens of studies is that objective life circumstances, once we've adapted to them, bear little relation to people's happiness. At one extreme, people with disabilities—even those paralyzed after car accidents—typically recover normal levels of day-to-day happiness. At the other extreme, people who've won a state lottery also settle back to their characteristic level of happiness.

Consider, too, how we have "made it." In 1957, per-person income, expressed in today's dollars, was less than $8,000. Today it is $16,000. With doubled incomes, we (at least those not left behind by the growing gap between rich and poor) now have double the material goods that money can buy—including twice as many cars per person. We also have microwave ovens, color TVs, VCRs, answering machines, and $12 billion a year worth of brand-name athletic shoes.

So are we indeed happier? We are not. In 1957, 35 percent of Americans told the National Opinion Research Center they were "very happy." In 1991, only 31 percent said the same. Meanwhile, depression rates have soared.

Ergo, wealth is like health: Although its utter absence breeds misery, having it is no guarantee of happiness. There is no need to envy the rich. Happiness is less a matter of getting what we want than wanting what we have.

Savor the moment. Happiness, said Benjamin Franklin, "is produced not so much by great pieces of good fortune that seldom happen as by the little advantages that occur every day."

As a future-oriented person, I periodically remind myself of Pascal's remark that we too often live as if the present were merely our means to the future. "So we never live, but we hope to live—and as we are always preparing to be happy, it is inevitable we should never be so."

To live in the present means, for me, taking delight in the day's magic moments, from morning tea and cereal, hunched over a manuscript, to the day's last moments, snuggling and talking with my wife. Happiness isn't somewhere off in the future, but in this morning's phone conversation with someone seeking advice, in this noon's meal with a friend, in this evening's bedtime story with a child, in tonight's curling up with a good book.

Take control of your time. There is, nevertheless, a place for setting goals and managing time. Compared to those who've learned a sense of helplessness, those with an "internal locus of control" do better in school, cope better with stress, and live with greater well-being. Deprived of control over one's life—an experience studied in prisoners, nursing home patients, and people living under totalitarian regimes—people suffer lower morale and poorer health.

One way to feel more empowered is to master our use of time. For happy people, time is "filled and planned," says Oxford University psychologist Michael Argyle. "For unhappy people time is unfilled, open and uncommitted; they postpone things and are inefficient."

To manage time effectively, set big goals, and then break them down into daily aims. Writing a book is, for me, too formidable and remote a goal. But writing two manuscript pages a day is easy enough. Repeat this little process 300 times over and, presto!, you have a book. Although we often overestimate how much we will accomplish in any given day (leaving us frustrated), we generally underestimate how much we can accomplish in a year, given just a little progress every day. Moreover, as each mini-deadline is met we get the delicious, confident feeling of being in control.

Act happy. As I stated in my previous article, study after study reveals three traits (in addition to the above-mentioned personal control) that mark happy people's lives. First, they like themselves. They exhibit self-esteem by agreeing with such statements as "I'm a lot of fun to be with" and "I have good ideas." Second, they are positive thinkers. Writing from a place called Hope [College], it is fitting that I concede the power of hope-filled optimism. Third, they are outgoing. We could imagine opposite findings—that introverts would be happiest, living in peaceful solitude, or that pessimists would live with greater gladness as things keep turning out better than expected. But it's the sociable extroverts and the venturesome optimists who report more happiness.

Although self-esteem, optimism, and extroversion tend to be enduring traits, those who seek greater happiness can exploit one of social psychology's arch principles: We are as likely to act ourselves into a way of thinking as to think ourselves into action. In experiments, people who feign high self-esteem begin feeling better about themselves. Even when manipulated into a smiling expression, people feel better; when they scowl, the whole world seems to scowl back. So put on a happy face. Pretend optimism. Simulate outgoingness. Going through the motions can trigger the emotions.

Seek work and leisure that engage your skills. Sometimes the challenges of work or home are too great, and we feel stressed. At other times, we're underchallenged and bored. In between these two states is a zone where we feel challenged, but not overmatched. We get absorbed. We lose consciousness of time. We are in a state that University of Chicago psychologist Mihaly Csikszentmihalyi calls "flow."

In his studies of writers, dancers, surgeons, chess players, mountain climbers, and the like, Csikszentmihalyi discovered that people find the flow experience satisfying. Even if we make a lower but livable wage, it pays to seek work that we find interesting and challenging.

The well-being that accompanies flow extends to leisure. Ironically, some of the most expensive forms of leisure are least likely to provide flow. Catch people sitting on a yacht or watching their big screen TV, and they typically don't feel all that great, for their skills aren't engaged. Catch them gardening, socializing, or writing a letter and you will likely find them feeling less apathetic and happier.

So off your duffs, couch potatoes. Pick up your camera. Tune that instrument. Sharpen those woodworking tools. Get out those quilting needles. Inflate the family basketball. Pull down a stimulating book. Oil the fishing reel. It's time to head out to the garden store. To invite friends over for tea. To pull down the Scrabble game. To go for a drive. Rather than vegetating in self-focused idleness, lose yourself in the flow of active work and play. "In every part and corner of our life, to lose oneself is to be a gainer," noted Robert Louis Stevenson. "To forget oneself is to be happy."

Join the "Movement" Movement. A slew of studies reveal that aerobic exercise is an antidote for mild depression and anxiety. Repeated surveys show that people are more self-confident, unstressed, and in better spirits, if physically fit.

The new exercise research is producing such consistent and encouraging results and with such minimal cost and desirable side effects that most people seeking to boost their energy and well-being can benefit from at least a moderate regimen. Chuck, my 76-year-old friend, plays basketball daily with people half his age and younger. "If I don't exercise five times a week," he explains, "I begin to get the blahs. The stamina I get from exercising helps keep me optimistic about living." *"Mens sana in corpore sano."* Sound mind in a sound body.

Get rest. Happy people live active, vigorous lives, yet they reserve time for renewing sleep and solitude. Today, however, many people suffer from shortened sleep, leaving them groggy and unable to get into flow. William Dement, director of Stanford University's Sleep Disorders Center, laments the "national sleep debt." Among the college students I have spent my adult life with, few behaviors strike me as more self-destructive than the typical late nights, with resulting fatigue, diminished alertness, and, not infrequently, failure and depression.

Poor time-management is part of the problem. Each diversion—a video game here, a bull session there, seems harmless enough. Yet, gradually, without intending sleeplessness, fatigue, and failure, the student veers toward falling behind and suffering the inevitable results.

A basic ingredient of energized, cheerful living is, therefore, to make time for enough sleep to awaken refreshed. In one study of Los Angeles County residents, people who made time for seven to eight hours sleep a night were not as likely to be depressed as those sleeping less (or more).

Research has even shown that a literal day of "REST"—that is, Restricted Environmental Stimulation Therapy—can work wonders. After a day of quiet on a comfortable bed in a dark, soundproofed room, people often emerge refreshed and with new self-control—an improved ability to stop smoking, to reduce drinking, to lose weight. Smaller doses of solitude, even a daily few minutes of meditation or prayer, can provide spiritual recharging for active living,

Give priority to close relationships. There are few better antidotes for unhappiness than an intimate friendship with someone who cares deeply about you. People who can name several close, supportive friends—friends with whom they freely share their ups and downs—live with greater health and happiness. In experiments, people relax as they confide painful experiences. Like confession, confiding is good for the soul.

Sadly, our increasingly individualistic society suffers from impoverished social connections, which some psychologists believe is a cause of today's epidemic levels of depression. As of 1993, 24 percent of Americans live alone, up from 8 percent a half-century ago. Compared to 1960, the divorce rate has doubled. The proportion of children not living with two parents has more than doubled, to nearly 3 in 10. This is, as Ronald Reagan proclaimed, "the age of the individual."

In contrast to the interdependence valued in Asian societies, Americans celebrate independence: Be true to yourself. Seek your own bliss. Be authentically you. And don't be (shudder) codependent (by supporting, loving, and staying tied to a troubled partner). Humanistic psychologist Carl Rogers epitomized today's individualism: "The only question which matters is, 'Am I living in a way which is deeply satisfying to me, and which truly expresses me?'"

Actually, that's not all that matters. A consensus is emerging from cross-cultural studies of individualism vs. collectivism, from gender scholarship on independence vs. connectedness, and from the new communitarian affirmation of shared values: to preserve our social fabric we need to balance me-thinking with we-thinking. The social ties that bind also provide support in difficult times.

For more than nine in 10 people, a significant close relationship is marriage. With other social bonds, broken marital relationships are a source of much unhappiness, while a supportive, committed companion is among life's greatest joys. To paraphrase Henry Ward Beecher, "a well-married person is winged; ill-matched, shackled." Three of four married people say their spouse is their best friend.

That helps explain why, during the 1970s and '80s, 39 percent of married adults (compared to only 24 percent of never-married adults) told the National Opinion Research Center they were "very happy." Without denying that divorce is sometimes a first step toward healing for those trapped in miserable relationships, a mountain of accumulating data reveal the benefits of an enduring, equitable, affectionate marriage.

So, don't forever shy away from commitment. If you're already married, resolve to nurture your relationship, to not take your partner for granted, to display to your spouse the sort of kindness that you display to others, to affirm your partner, to play together and share together. Resolve in such ways to act lovingly, and you both may find your affections rejuvenated.

Take care of the soul. "Joy is the serious business of heaven," said C. S. Lewis. One surmises as much from reading the new research on faith and well-being. Actively religious people are much less likely to become delinquent, to abuse drugs and alcohol, to divorce, or to commit suicide. They're even physically healthier, due perhaps to less smoking and drinking.

In Europe and North America, religiously active people are also happier. In one Gallup survey, highly spiritual people (who, for example, agree that "My religious faith is the most important influence in my life") were twice as likely, as those lowest in spiritual commitment, to declare themselves "very happy." In study after study, elderly people as well express more satisfaction with their lives if religiously active.

Other studies suggest that faith "buffers" a crisis. Those who've recently suffered divorce, unemployment, bereavement, or disability report greater well-being if they have a strong religious faith. Compared to religiously inactive widows, widows who worship regularly report more joy in their lives. Mothers of children with disabilities are less vulnerable to depression if sustained by a religious faith.

Faith doesn't promise immunity from suffering. But it does enable a strengthened walk through valleys of darkness. For many people, a religious faith places them within a network of social support—one of America's

294,000 local churches and synagogues. Their faith helps them define life's meaning and purpose. It enables feelings of ultimate acceptance. It motivates a focus beyond self (reflected in Gallup's report of doubled rates of charitable giving and volunteerism among weekly church attendees compared to non-attendees). And it offers a timeless spiritual perspective on the great enemy, death, and all of life's other woes.

Such psychological factors don't bear on the truth of any religious claim. But they have nudged more than a few people to take the leap of faith.

Digested from The Pursuit of Happiness *(Avon Books; 1993) by David G. Myers, Ph.D. Copyright 1993 by the David and Carol Myers Foundation.*

Psychology Today Magazine, Jul/Aug 1993
Psychology Today © Copyright 1991-2008

Lesson 5
The Big Picture

Introduction

Do you ever feel like you keep dealing with the same problems over and over again? Does life feel like you are running on a treadmill to nowhere, where you need to keep moving just to stay in the same place? If you are trying to get across town, a treadmill is a very poor means of transportation. But if your goal is developing stamina or getting into a shape, a treadmill is quite an effective device.

In this lesson you'll learn to consider your recurring personal struggle in the larger framework of the universe at large. You may never become perfect. But perhaps even an imperfect person can contribute to the making of a perfect world.

Action Is the Main Thing
The Irresolvable Conflict

Learning Exercise 1

It's Monday morning, and as you stumble into the kitchen in search of your morning coffee, you realize that you are all out. You don't feel like a person until you've had your caffeine fix, so you are one unhappy camper. You really wish you had a nice steaming cup in your hand right now. Your spouse, who knows just how you feel about coffee and enjoys a good cup too, comes into the kitchen and sympathizes with you. Together, you talk about how good a cup of French vanilla roast would taste, favorite coffee shops you have visited, and how challenging it is to start the day without coffee. Soon, you are feeling a bit better, and sit down for breakfast. Suddenly, your teenaged daughter enters the kitchen with a bag. She can't stand coffee herself, but she overheard you talking, so she ran down to the corner store and brought a hot cup home for you.

Compare and contrast what your spouse has done for you and what your daughter has done for you.

Who has a better understanding of why you want a cup of coffee?

Who shares your feelings about coffee more deeply?

Text 1

להבין מעט מזעיר תכלית בריאת הבינונים וירידת נשמותיהם לעוה״ז . . .

מאחר שלא יוכלו לשלחה כל ימיהם . . .

רק שלבושיה אינם מתלבשים בגופם . . .

ואם כן למה זה ירדו נשמותיהם לעוה״ז

ליגע לריק ח״ו להלחם כל ימיהם עם היצר ולא יכלו לו

Let us understand . . . the purpose of the creation of *beinonim* and their souls' descent into the world . . . . Since they will not be able to eradicate [the animal soul] throughout their lives . . . but only [ensure] that its garments do not invest themselves in their bodies . . . . If so, why have their souls descended into this world to labor in vain . . . to wage war throughout their lives against this nature which they cannot vanquish?

TANYA, CHAPTER 35

Consolation to the *Beinoni*

Oil, Wick, and Flame

Learning Exercise 2

Complete the following chart, using the information in Text 2 to help you.

The Metaphor of the Oil Lamp

Physical Model	Spiritual Counterpart
Oil	
Wick	
Flame	
Burning	

ותהי זאת נחמתם והוא בהקדים לשון הינוקא
[בזהר] . . . בגין דגופא דב"נ איהו פתילה . . .
דהא נהורא דבראשו אצטריך למשחא ואינון עובדאן טבאן
. . . והנה ביאור משל זה שהמשיל אור השכינה לאור הנר
שאינו מאיר ונאחז בפתילה בלי שמן
וכך אין השכינה שורה על גוף האדם שנמשל לפתילה
אלא ע"י מעשים טובים דווקא ולא די לו בנשמתו . . .
להיות היא כשמן לפתילה . . .
כי הנה נשמת האדם אפילו הוא צדיק גמור
. . . אף על פי כן אינה בטילה במציאות לגמרי
ליבטל וליכלל באור ה' ממש להיות לאחדים ומיוחדים ביחוד גמור
רק הוא דבר בפני עצמו ירא ה' ואוהבו.
משא"כ המצות ומעשים טובים . . .
אין החיות שבהם דבר נפרד בפני עצמו כלל
אלא הוא מיוחד ונכלל ברצונו ית'
והיו לאחדים ממש ביחוד גמור

But let this be the consolation [to the *beinoni*] . . . . To quote the *Zohar* . . . "The body of a man is a wick . . . and the Light [which shines] on a man's head needs oil, meaning good deeds . . . ."

The Light of G-d's Presence is compared to the flame of a lamp, which does not shine nor cling to the wick without oil. Likewise, the [light of] G-d's Presence does not rest on a man's body, which is likened to a wick, without good deeds [as fuel].

It is not sufficient that his soul . . . should act for him as oil for the wick . . . . [because] the soul of a person, even of a perfect *tsadik* . . . does not completely dissolve itself out of existence so as to be truly nullified and absorbed into the Light of G-d to the extent of becoming one and the same absolutely. Rather, the person remains an entity apart, who feels awe for G-d and loves Him. It is different, however, with the commandments and good deeds . . . . The vitality that is within them is in no way a separate, independent thing but is united and absorbed within His blessed will, and they become truly one in a perfect union.

TANYA, CHAPTER 35

How It Works

Figure 1

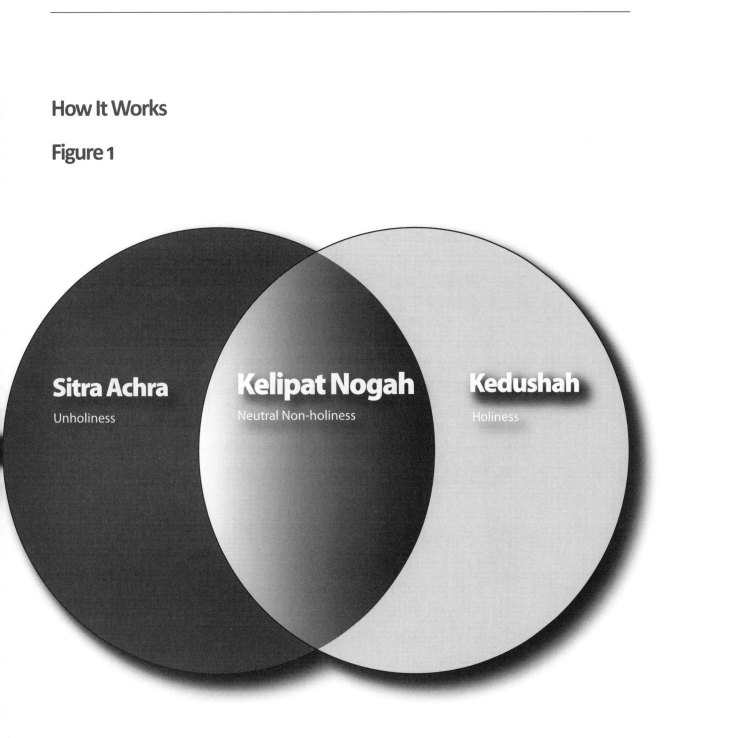

Sitra Achra
Unholiness

Kelipat Nogah
Neutral Non-holiness

Kedushah
Holiness

Text 3

והנה כשהאדם עוסק בתורה

אזי נשמתו שהיא נפשו האלהית עם שני לבושיה הפנימים לבדם

שהם כח הדבור ומחשבה נכללות באור ה' א"ס ב"ה

ומיוחדות בו ביחוד גמור . . .

אך כדי להמשיך אור והארת השכינה גם על גופו ונפשו הבהמית

שהיא החיונית המלובשת בגופו ממש

צריך לקיים מצות מעשיות הנעשים ע"י הגוף ממש

שאז כח הגוף ממש שבעשיה זו נכלל באור ה' ורצונו ומיוחד בו ביחוד גמור . . .

ואזי גם כח נפש החיונית שבגופו ממש שמקליפת נוגה

נתהפך מרע לטוב ונכלל ממש בקדושה . . .

מאחר שהוא הוא הפועל ועושה מעשה המצוה

. . . ואף שמהותה ועצמותה של נפש הבהמית

עדיין לא נכללו בקדושה מ"מ מאחר דאתכפין לקדושה . . .

ומתרצין לעשיית המצוה . . .

דהיינו שכח נפש החיונית המלובש בעשיית המצוה

הוא נכלל ממש באור ה' ומיוחד בו ביחוד גמור

In order to draw the light of G-d's Presence over his body he needs to fulfill commandments which are performed by the body itself. Thereby, the very energy of the body itself which is engaged in this action is absorbed . . . and united with [G-d] in a perfect union.

Tanya, Chapter 35

Text 4

והנה מודעת זאת מארז״ל
שתכלית בריאת עולם הזה
הוא שנתאוה הקב״ה להיות לו דירה בתחתונים

I t is a well-known saying of our Sages that the purpose of the creation of this world, is that G-d yearned to have a home in the lower worlds.

TANYA, CHAPTER 36

Text 5

והנה תכלית השלימות . . . תלוי במעשינו ועבודתנו . . .
כי הגורם שכר המצוה היא המצוה בעצמה

T he ultimate perfection [of this world which will exist in] the Messianic era and [the time of] the resurrection of the dead, meaning the revelation of the Infinite Light in this physical world, is dependent on our actions and service throughout the period of exile. For it is the *mitzvah* itself that generates its own reward.

TANYA, CHAPTER 37

Objects

Text 6

כי בעשייתה ממשיך האדם גילוי אור א"ס ב"ה מלמעלה למטה
להתלבש בגשמיות עוה"ז בדבר שהיה תחלה תחת ממשלת קליפת נוגה . . .
כגון קלף התפילין ומזוזה וספר תורה . . . וכן אתרוג שאינו ערלה . . .
ומעות הצדקה שאינן גזל וכיוצא בהם
ועכשיו שמקיים בהם מצות ה' ורצונו
הרי החיות שבהם עולה ומתבטל ונכלל באור א"ס ב"ה
שהוא רצונו ית' המלובש בהם
מאחר שאין שם בחי' הסתר פנים כלל להסתיר אורו ית'

By performing [a *mitzvah*] the person draws the revelation of the blessed Infinite Light from above downwards, to be clothed in the physicality of this world, in an object which had heretofore been under the dominion of non-holiness . . . . for example, the parchment of the tefilin, mezuzah and Torah scroll . . . . Similarly, an etrog which is not *orlah* [the forbidden fruit of a tree's first three harvests], or money given to charity that has not been acquired through theft, and the like. Now that one fulfills G-d's commandment and will with these objects, the vitality within them ascends and is dissolved and absorbed into the blessed Infinite Light, which is His will that is expressed in the *mitzvot*. For [in a *mitzvah*] there is nothing whatsoever to hide His light.

TANYA, CHAPTER 37

Energy of the Animal Soul

Text 7 📜

וכן כח נפש החיונית הבהמית שבאברי גוף האדם המקיים המצוה

הוא מתלבש ג"כ בעשיה זו ועולה מהקליפה ונכלל בקדושת המצוה

. . . גם במצות תלמוד תורה וק"ש ותפלה וכיוצא בהן

אף שאינן בעשיה גשמית ממש . . .

מ"מ הא קיימא לן דהרהור לאו כדבור דמי

ואינו יוצא ידי חובתו עד שיוציא בשפתיו . . .

כי אי אפשר לנפש האלהית לבטא בשפתיים ופה ולשון ושיניים הגשמיים

כי אם ע"י נפש החיונית הבהמית המלובשת באברי הגוף ממש

וכל מה שמדבר בכח גדול יותר

הוא מכניס ומלביש יותר כחות מנפש החיונית בדיבורים אלו

Similarly, the power of the vitalizing animal soul clothed in the bodily limbs of a person who performs a *mitzvah* clothes itself in the deed of the *mitzvah* and it ascends from non-holiness to be absorbed into the holiness of the *mitzvah* . . . . Even in the case of such [speech-related] *mitzvot* as Torah study, reciting the *Shema*, prayer and the like, although they do not involve actual physical action, yet one does not fulfill the duty [of Torah study, prayer, etc.] unless he actually utters [the words] with his lips.

TANYA, CHAPTER 37

Food, Drink, and Other Resources
that Support Human Life

Text 8 🕮

‫... מצות מעשיות הרי כל גידולו וחיותו מהדם ...‬
‫שהן כל אוכלין ומשקין שאכל ושתה ...שהיו תחת ממשלתה ...‬
‫ועתה היא מתהפכת מרע לטוב ...‬
‫וע"י זה תעלה ג"כ כללות קליפת נוגה‬
‫שהיא כללות החיות של עו"הז הגשמי והחומרי‬

The energy invested into the performance of *mitzvot* involving action derives its vitality from . . . all the food and drink that one has eaten and drunk. . . . These were under the dominion of non-holiness, [but when the person performs a *mitzvah* with the energy derived from this food and drink] this non-holiness is transformed. . . . Thereby all of the realm of neutral non-holiness, which constitutes the vitality of this physical world as a whole, will ascend as well.

TANYA, CHAPTER 37

Text 9

כי כל תכלית של ימות המשיח ותחיית המתים
שהוא גילוי כבודו ואלקותו ית'
ולהעביר רוח הטומאה מן הארץ תלוי בהמשכת אלקותו
. . . ע"י קיומה כל רמ"ח מצות עשה
ולהעביר רוח הטומאה ממנה בשמירת' כל שס"ה מצות ל"ת
שלא יינקו ממנה שס"ה גידיה
כי כללות ישראל שהם ששים רבוא נשמות פרטיות
הם כללות החיות של כללות העולם כי בשבילם נברא
וכל פרט מהם הוא כולל ושייך לו החיות של חלק אחד מששים רבוא
מכללות העולם התלוי בנפשו החיונית להעלותו לה' בעלייתה
דהיינו במה שמשתמש מעוה"ז לצורך גופו ונפשו החיונית
לעבודת ה' כגון אכילה ושתיה ודומיהם ודירה וכל כלי תשמישיו

The era of Mashiach and of the resurrection—namely, the time of revelation of G‑d's glory and divinity in this world and the banishment of the spirit of impurity from the earth—is entirely dependent on our drawing down His G‑dliness . . . through performance of the *mitzvot* . . . .

Each soul is related to the vitality of [a proportionate] fraction of the entire world, and this [portion of the world] depends on that vital soul for its elevation, by means of his partaking of this world for the requirements of his body and vital soul in the service of G‑d. For example: eating, drinking, and the like; one's dwelling and all his possessions.

Tanya, Chapter 37

Text 10

כי זה כל האדם ותכלית בריאתו וירידתו לעוה״ז
להיות לו ית׳ דירה בתחתונים דוקא
לאהפכא חשוכא לנהורא
וימלא כבוד ה׳ את כל הארץ הגשמית דייקא וראו כל בשר יחדיו

For, "This is man's entire purpose," the purpose for which he was created and for which [his soul] descended to this world, so that G-d may have an abode precisely in the lowest realms, to turn the darkness of this world into light so that G-d's glory will fill the entire physical world and: "All flesh will see [G-dliness] together (Yeshayahu/Isaiah 40:5)."

TANYA, CHAPTER 37

Learning Exercise 3

Select a favorite *mitzvah*, and imagine you needed to perform this *mitzvah* on another planet.

1. Working with a partner, list all the things you would need to take along because they are directly needed for performing the *mitzvah*.

2. Now list all the things you need to take along because they are necessary resources for the items on you listed in the first part of the exercise.

Try to be as thorough as possible in your responses.

Figure 2: The Ripple Effect of A *Mitzvah*

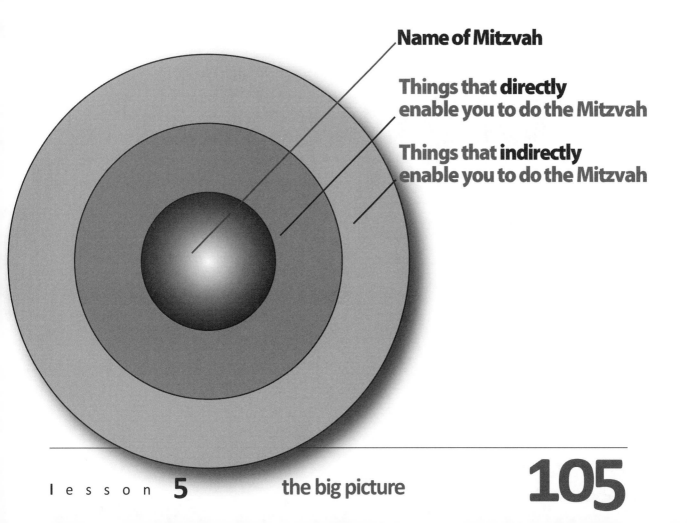

Name of Mitzvah

Things that directly enable you to do the Mitzvah

Things that indirectly enable you to do the Mitzvah

Intent
Body and Soul

Text 11

אך אעפ״כ אמרו תפלה או שאר ברכה בלא כוונה
הן כגוף בלא נשמה

Nevertheless, it has been said that, "Prayer, or any other blessing, said without *kavanah*, is like a soulless body [Rabbi Isaiah Hurwitz, *Shenei Luchot ha-Berit*, vol. 1, p. 249b]."

TANYA, CHAPTER 38

Text 12 🔖

ולא שדביקות המחשבה

. . . היא מצד עצמה למעלה מדביקות קיום המצות מעשי׳ . . .

אלא . . . שזהו ג״כ רצונו ית׳ לדבקה בשכל ומחשבה וכוונת המצות מעשי׳ . . .

והארת רצון העליון . . . המאירה ומלובשת בכוונה זו היא גדולה לאין קץ . . .

מהארת רצון העליון המאירה ומלובשת בקיום המצות עצמן

במעשה ובדבור בלי כוונה כגודל מעלת אור הנשמה על הגוף

שהוא כלי ומלבוש הנשמה כמו גוף המצוה

שהוא כלי ומלבוש לכוונתה

Not that [*kavanah*] is intrinsically superior to the action of *mitzvot*.... Rather it is also His blessed will that one should cleave to Him with one's intelligence, thought and intention in the active commandments .... And the illumination ... which irradiates and pervades this *kavanah* is infinitely greater and more sublime than the illumination ... which irradiates and pervades the performance of the commandments themselves in action and speech without *kavanah*. It is comparable to the superiority of the light of the soul over the body, which is a vessel and garb for the soul, as the body of the commandment is a vessel and garb for its *kavanah*.

Tanya, Chapter 38

Levels of Intent (Optional Section)

Text 13

וכוונת המצות . . . נחלקת . . . לשתי מדרגות כמו שתי מדרגות הנשמה
שהן בגוף החומרי שהן חי ומדבר
כי מי שדעתו יפה לדעת את ה' ולהתבונן בגדולתו ית'
ולהוליד מבינתו יראה עילאה . . .
ואהבת ה' . . . להיות נפשו צמאה לה' לדבקה בו ע"י קיום התורה והמצות . . .
הרי כוונה זו על ד"מ כמו נשמת המדבר שהוא בעל שכל ובחירה ובדעת ידבר
ומי שדעתו קצרה לידע ולהתבונן בגדולת א"ס ב"ה
להוליד האהבה מבינתו בהתגלות לבו וכן היראה במוחו ופחד ה' בלבו
רק שזוכר ומעורר את האהבה הטבעית המסותרת בלבו
ומוציאה . . . אל הגילוי במוח
. . . הרי כוונה זו עד"מ כמו נשמת החי שאינו בעל שכל ובחירה
וכל מדותיו שהן יראתו מדברים המזיקים אותו
ואהבתו לדברים הנאהבים אצלו
הן רק טבעיים אצלו ולא מבינתו ודעתו
וכך הן על ד"מ היראה והאהבה הטבעיות המסותרות בלב כל ישראל
כי הן ירושה לנו מאבותינו וכמו טבע בנפשותינו כנז"ל

The *kavanah* of *mitzvot . . .* is divided into two levels corresponding to the two levels of souls present in material bodies, namely in animals, and in man. [The first level is that of] a person discerning enough to know G-d and to reflect on His greatness, and to create out of his understanding a lofty awe . . . and love of G-d . . . so that his soul thirsts for G-d, [seeking] to cleave to Him by fulfilling the Torah and *mitzvot . . . .* Such *kavanah* is analogous to the soul of a human being, who possesses intelligence and freedom of choice and who speaks with wisdom.

As for a person whose understanding is too limited to know and to reflect on the greatness of the blessed Infinite, so as to create out of his understanding a revealed love in his heart, and also awe in his mind and dread of G-d in his heart: rather, he merely recalls and arouses the natural love hidden in his heart and brings it into a state of consciousness in his mind . . . . [Such *kavanah*] is analogous to the soul of an animal, which possesses neither intelligence nor freedom of choice, and whose emotions—its fear of harmful things and its love of pleasing things—are merely natural to it, not of its intelligence or understanding.

So, too, by way of example, are the natural love and awe hidden in the heart of every Jew; for they are our inheritance from our patriarchs, and are like a natural instinct in our souls, as mentioned previously.

TANYA, CHAPTER 38

Wings

Text 14 📖

ובזה יובן היטב הא דדחילו ורחימו נקראי׳ גדפין . . .
כי כמו שכנפי העוף אינם עיקר העוף ואין חיותו תלוי בהם כלל
כדתנן ניטלו אגפיה כשרה
והעיקר הוא ראשו וכל גופו והכנפיי׳ אינם רק משמשים לראשו וגופו לפרחא בהון
וכך ד״מ התורה ומצות הן עיקר היחוד העליון
ע״י גילוי רצון העליון המתגלה על ידיהן
והדחילו ורחימו הם מעלים אותן למקום שיתגלה בו הרצון אור אין סוף ברוך הוא
והיחוד שהן יצירה ובריאה

This explains clearly why awe and love are figuratively called "wings" . . . . The wings of a bird are not its main components; its life does not depend on them at all. Rather, the main parts are its head and the rest of its body; the wings merely serve the head and body, enabling them to fly.

Likewise with Torah and *mitzvot*: They constitute the essential supernal union by the revelation of supernal will which they cause. Awe and love [merely] elevate the Torah and *mitzvot* to a place where this will—the blessed Infinite Light—and this unity can be revealed.

TANYA, CHAPTER 40

Optional Text A

In light of the above, we can understand why our Sages so greatly extolled the virtue of charity, declaring it equal to all the other *mitzvot* together . . . . For the purpose of all these *mitzvot* is only to elevate one's animal soul to G-d, since it is this vital soul that performs them [*mitzvot*] and clothes itself in them, so as to be absorbed into the blessed Infinite Light clothed in them. Now, you will find no other *mitzvah* in which the vital soul is clothed to the same extent as in the *mitzvah* of charity. For in all other *mitzvot* only one faculty of the vital soul is clothed only while the *mitzvah* is being performed. In the case of charity, however, which one gives from [the proceeds] of the toil of his hands, surely all the strength of his vital soul is clothed in (i.e., applied to) the effort of his labor, or in any other occupation by which he earned this money.

Thus when he gives to charity this money, his entire vital soul ascends to G-d. Even he who does not earn his livelihood from his labors, nevertheless, since he could have purchased with this money that he gave for charity, sustenance for the life of his vital soul, he is actually giving his soul's life to G-d in the form of charity. Thus, charity comprises and therefore elevates more energy of the vital soul than any other *mitzvah*. This is why our Sages have said that charity hastens the Messianic redemption: For with one act of charity one elevates a great deal of the vital soul; more of its faculties and powers, in fact, than he might elevate through many other active *mitzvot* [combined].

TANYA, CHAPTER 37

Key Points

1. Man's microcosmic struggle towards inner perfection is mirrored in the world's macrocosmic struggle towards external perfection.

2. Action is central, and more important than spiritual "enlightenment." Thus, even the imperfect person is able to engage meaningfully in life's most important purpose.

3. *Mitzvot* elevate "neutral non-holiness" into holiness, thereby building the "G-dly dwelling in the lower realms," which is the purpose of our creation.

4. The natural result of *mitzvot* is the transformation and elevation of the world to G-dliness, culminating in the perfect world described by our prophets as the end-point of our service to G-d.

5. A *mitzvah* elevates the animal soul as well as the food, drink and other resources expended for its purpose.

6. Intent, constituting the feelings of love and awe, adds energy and life to our actions and intensifies the effect of the *mitzvah*.

7. A *mitzvah* is compared to a bird, and the intent to its wings.

Additional Readings

The Abnormality of Jewish Life

by **Dr. Yaakov Brawer**

"Can't you do anything normal?" The first time I heard this question actually voiced was 15 years ago. I was a newly appointed member of the staff of the Royal Victoria Hospital and of McGill University. I had walked out in the middle of an important departmental budget meeting because the sun was low, it was *Tu B'Shevat* (the 15th of the Jewish month of Shevat, celebrated as the "New Year for Trees"), and I had yet to eat any fruit.

I ran down Peel Street to Chabad House, ate a couple of figs, and ran back to the hospital, where I was confronted by several concerned colleagues who naturally assumed that my abrupt exit from such an urgent meeting betokened the onset of serious illness. I put their minds at rest and told them about *Tu B'Shevat*, the sun and the figs. They looked at me in frustrated disbelief, and one of them, a Jew, sputtered the question that had probably been gnawing at him since my arrival at McGill: "Can't you do anything normal?"

Aside from the grammar, it was an excellent question. It encompassed absences from important professional activities on Shabbat and Jewish Holidays, unwillingness to attend obligatory social events such as the rash of holiday parties in late December, the beard, *tzitzit*, dietary restrictions, etc. The answer is, of course, No. I can't do anything normal. Jewish life is simply not normal. The Torah demands abnormality.

Normality is a state of being that is largely misunderstood and the term, therefore, is often misapplied. Normality implies predictability and harmony with nature. Such a condition usually engenders positive feelings. We feel comfortable and secure when our physician tells us that our test results are normal, or when the principal assures us that our wayward child's behavior, although irritating,

is that of a normal teenager. People intuitively equate normal with good. In fact, normal is very bad.

Let's consider, for a minute, the physician's assurance that one's health is normal. What he/she really means is the exact opposite. That a single cell in the body is able to perform and coordinate the vast complex of biochemical operations required in order to simply be classified as "alive" is not only not normal, but is so improbable as to statistically approach impossibility. Add to this orders of magnitude in intricacy that describe the interactions of individual cells in tissues and organs, and you are confronted with nothing short of a miracle. There is nothing more abnormal than an individual whose body functions properly. Illness, deterioration, and death, on the other hand, are natural, predictable, and are very much favored by the innate rules governing physical existence.

The ultimate fact of life in this universe is the second law of thermodynamics. Crudely put, it states that things run down--they do not run up. Energy tends to dissipate; structure and order tend to deteriorate into randomness. This is normal. According to the second law of thermodynamics, a person achieves ultimate harmony with nature when he is dead and the molecules that comprised his being are in thermodynamic equilibrium with the environment, which is to say he is dust.

The second law of thermodynamics can be opposed, albeit at a very high cost. People instinctively know this. Someone, for example, who needs a car, will not wander about in the wilderness looking for one, in the expectation that a functional car has materialized spontaneously somewhere, in response to the random forces of nature. A car, after all, represents a highly abnormal state of being. In order to develop a car from a pile of iron ore, a great deal of energy must be spent since the formless heap of metal ore is in a relatively stable natural state in comparison to the highly ordered, unnatural and exceedingly improbable structure that constitutes a car. Cars, therefore, cost. The reverse process, however, costs nothing. For a car to deteriorate into a random heap of metal is normal, as every car owner well knows. The more unnatural a structure, the greater is the expenditure of energy (the cost) required to produce it.

The same principle governs all of worldly being. From whatever perspective one chooses, biochemistry, economics, sociology, cosmology, etc.--purpose and order are anomalous and, therefore, energy must be expended in order to achieve these improbable, unstable, and preternatural conditions. The fundamental principle described by the second law of thermodynamics is thus applicable, in one form or another, to every facet of our lives.

How we relate to this all-encompassing reality determines how we spend our lives. As in the case of any law, one can choose to conform or to resist. The Jews have chosen to resist with a vengeance, thus earning for themselves well-deserved notoriety as a "stiff-necked people."

What is the connection between turning a lump of iron ore into a car and the peculiar behavior of the Jews? How and why do Jews battle the natural order? In order to answer these questions, it is first necessary to consider a more basic problem. What is the natural order and why was it created to begin with?

The answer is expressed, in metaphoric terms, in the Midrash (Tanchuma, Nasso 7:1). " G-d desired a residence in the lower worlds."

Although at first glance, this cryptic statement doesn't seem to explain anything, in fact, it explains everything. Moreover, we are already thoroughly familiar with "lower worlds" because that's where we happen to live. The lowest of the "lower worlds" is the physical universe. The expression "below" or "lower worlds" conveys several important ideas. First of all, it implies that there is an "above" or "upper worlds." Secondly, in the context of the statement in Midrash, "below" is a state of being that is preferable to, and therefore, potentially superior to that described as "above."

"Below" and "above" are clearly not spatial designations, but rather refer to stages or levels in the process of creation. For example, a person may at some point in his life become aware of the fact that he wants a house. He then finds reasons why having a house is an excellent idea:

it's a good investment, his family is getting larger, etc. Subsequently he imagines what sort of a house he would like. He then hires an architect to design the house, and so on until he actually has the house. What was first a pure, amorphous desire evolved into a process of reasoning. This gave rise to a mental abstraction of the house that was later developed into a physical abstraction (the architect's blueprints).

The creative process, therefore, consists of a dynamic chain of cause and effect in which "higher" elements, e.g., the person's mental image, are antecedent to lower levels such as the blueprints. Obviously the lowest level in this chain, the ultimate in "below," is the house itself and it is only this absolute lowest stage that satisfies the primal will that initiated the entire process. The mental images and blueprints, although expressions of creativity and imagination, do not satisfy. Their sole *raison d'être is* that they are necessary steps leading to the fulfillment of the original will.

In a similar vein, the process of Divine creation comprises a progressive series of stages one "below" the next. The ultimate goal is the lowest stage, in which the primordial Divine will, that initiated the entire process, can be finally realized.

The stages are referred to as "worlds". In Hebrew, the word for "world" is *olam* which is etymologically related to the word *he'elem*, meaning concealment. The Divine creative process consists of a progressive sequence of condensations, or concealments, in which each stage or "world" evolves into the next lower stage. With each succeeding step (world) the Divine vitalizing force becomes more obscured, such that the lower you go, the more limited, independent, and distinct from its source each world appears. As in the house analogy, higher worlds (although more transparent to the Divinity that animates them) have no intrinsic significance. The evolutionary chain of spiritual worlds are important only as means through which the original Divine will can be ultimately actualized in the final stage, which is the physical world, or universe in which we live.

Our world is the end of the line, "below" which there is nothing else. It is, therefore, the "location" in which G-d desires a residence. The question now is what is a "residence" and how can this world possibly qualify as such a place?

Offhand, the concept of a residence for G-d sounds idolatrous. The crude man-gods of mythology had residences. Zeus lived on Olympus, Odin in Valhalla and so forth. Of course, as in the case of the term "below," the expression "residence" is intended by the Midrash to be understood metaphorically. It is, however, not an easy metaphor to grasp. The concept of residence implies limitation. It excludes all aspects of existence (e.g., upper worlds) that do not conform to its specifications. How can G-d, who is infinite and who completely transcends creation, be contained by a facet of creation with finite dimensions? Moreover, the entire creation, upper and lower, is nothing more than an expression of G-d's unlimited will and wisdom, and is, therefore, totally dependent upon and negated to Him, just as a person's thoughts have no existence independent of himself. Creation is contained within G-d (as a person's thought is contained within himself); G-d is not confined by creation. What then is meant by a "residence" for G-d?

The term actually tells us nothing about G-d's essence, which is absolutely unknowable, but rather something about how He wishes to manifest Himself. Consider what a residence means in human terms. An individual wakes up in the morning and goes off to work. At the office he reveals himself as a professional. His behavior patterns, speech, and social interactions all reflect the necessity of fulfilling the professional role. To his students (let's assume he is a professor) he is one thing, to his colleagues, something else, and to his chairman, something else again. At lunchtime he goes downtown to buy a coat and must then assume an entirely new and different identity, namely that of a customer. On the way back home on the subway he has to transform, once again, into another class of being characterized by its own unique behavior pattern. He becomes a passenger.

Supposing someone wanted to know who and what this person really is. Of all the images that he projects during the course of the day, which, if any, is really him? Is there not a circumstance in which this individual does not have to mold himself into some required role?

Catch him at home. In one's residence, one is free of the necessity of projecting any particular image. It is his refuge where he can be himself and reveal himself as he is. The idiom to "feel at home" conveys such a meaning. It implies total freedom of self-expression.

G-d desires to reveal his unified infinite essence specifically in this finite multifarious world. He would like His will to be openly reflected in the physical world and its creatures. Such, in fact, was the case in the Tabernacle or in the first Temple in which Divinity was openly revealed. Hence the Temple is referred to as the "house of G-d." Although all creation is an expression of G-dliness, it was only in the Temple that this was clear and obvious.

In the rest of creation, Divinity is obscured, just as the real identity of a person is obscured by the masks he assumes in playing the various roles required of him. G-d's essential will, which reflects His essence, is concealed by masks that we would call natural law. G-d's ultimate desire is that He be revealed not only in one restricted region of the world, such as in the Temple, but rather that the whole world reveal the essence of His Divinity, i.e., the whole world become His "residence."

This then is the meaning of the Midrashic statement that " G-d desired a residence in the lower worlds."

By now it should also be clear that such a desire is impossible to fulfill for the simple reason that "below" and "residence" are not only antithetical to one another, but each can exist only at the expense of the other. If there is a "below" there can be no "residence" since below is created by means of a progressive series of concealments, ultimately totally obscuring Divinity within the garments of nature. The world is not only opaque to G-dliness, it was created specifically by eclipsing G-dliness. Likewise, if there is a "residence," there can be no "below." G-d could very well reveal himself and in so doing remove all of the masks and garments in which he conceals Himself, thus eliminating the possibility of "worlds" and certainly of a world such as ours, which is seemingly totally independent of Him. If what the Midrash says is correct, what G-d demands is impossible, or at the very least exceedingly abnormal.

This seemingly insoluble paradox is appreciated by the philosophers and theologians of all nationalities and religions. There are clearly two very different realities—G-d and the world. Worldliness and G-dliness are irreconcilable and, therefore, one can attain one only at the expense of the other. Religious experience demands withdrawal from worldly life. In this sense, both the Catholic priest and the Buddhist monk are motivated by the same rationale. On the other hand, religious sensitivity is a definite drawback if one's aim in life is to rule Wall Street. In fact, a compromise can be hammered out. There can be times and places for pursuing Divinity, and other times and places for pursuing worldly ends. The proportion of time and effort spent in heavenly or in earthly pursuits is then determined by personal inclination. This is a philosophically sound approach that allows for a normal balanced life. The problem is that it is inconsistent with G-d's objective as propounded in the Midrash.

Contrary to all reason, the Jewish people have taken on the Divine task of converting this finite, physical world with all of its minutiae into a residence for G-d. If the conversion of a lump of iron into a car is abnormal and contrary to nature, how is one to view the conversion of a car into a vessel for revealing G-dliness? It is normal for a Scroll to reveal holiness just as it is for a car to reflect worldliness. For a car, or a house, or food to reveal G-dliness is unprecedented and totally beyond grasp. Nonetheless, this fusion of two mutually antithetical states of being into one reality is accomplished daily by Jews living Jewish lives.

How is it done? Simple. The directions are supplied in the Torah. The car is not driven on Shabbat, specifically because it is Shabbat. The house has *mezzuzahs* identifying it as a Jewish house and property of the Creator. The food is kosher and a *brachah* is recited before and after eating. The energy supplied by the food is used toward the service of G-d in learning Torah and performing mitzvot. The application of Torah and Mitzvot to each and every aspect of earthly existence transforms all worldly objects and affairs into vessels in which G-d's supernal will can be manifest. Thus, every mitzvah performed by every Jew produces another brick for G-d's residence.

The process has been slow and laborious. It is no accident that the word for Divine service, *avodah,* literally means work. Moreover, we have been engaged in this "work" for 3,300 years. There is little doubt, however, that the job is almost complete, and when it is, the G-dliness that is the life of all existence will be revealed in everything.

The Jew, then, cannot be normal. With his soul rooted in Divine will and his feet planted on the ground, he appears as an outsider in both heaven and earth. You want to be religious? Fine. Go sit in *shul* and study Torah. You want to be an active participant in modern worldly life? Also good. Find a lucrative, prestigious profession and get to work. But what has worldly life to do with G-d and G-d with worldly life? The answer, of course, is everything.

Reprinted with permission from chabad.org

Originally from *Wellsprings Magazine,* a journal of Jewish thought published by Lubavitch Youth Organization..

Why It's Frustrating to Have a Brain

by **Rabbi Yanki Tauber**

Having a brain means that you not only know how things are, but you also understand how things ought to be. Which means that you're constantly being made aware that things are not as they ought to be.

Human beings (most of whom have brains) deal with this frustration in a variety of ways. Some become "academics", which means that they concentrate on the way things ought to be and make believe that that's the way things are. Those who for some reason (usually job-related) are compelled to deal with the way things are, try not to think about the way things ought to be. Since neither approach can be maintained 100% of the time, human beings enjoy a higher stress level than cows, for example.

This has led humans to invent all sorts of salves and balms for stress, on the one hand, and all sorts of devices to do away with (or at least numb) the brain, on the other. Which is a shame, since it's great having a brain, and it's healthy to experience stress.

(Obviously, there are certain types of stress that are quite sick and disabling, but we're talking about the healthy, productive kind that's part and parcel of what being human is all about).

The Torah is very mincing with words. Laws whose details cover many pages in the Talmud are expressed by the Torah in a single sentence, a single word, or even a single extra letter. Little wonder: the "Written Torah" (as the Five Books of Moses are called) has less than 80,000 words (about the quantity of a good-sized novel) in which to encapsulate the whole of the Divine communication to man.

But when it comes to the Sanctuary made by the people of Israel in the Sinai Desert, the Torah does a very unusual thing: it elaborates. And then it elaborates some more. First we get a description of every one of the Sanctuary's components as spelled out in G-d's instructions to Moses. And then we get all the details a second time, in the account of the Sanctuary's actual construction. The most amazing thing is that these two descriptions are virtually identical! The only real difference is that in the first account, the description of each item begins, "And they shall make. . . ", and in the second account it begins, "And they made. . . "

The Sanctuary is the prototype of the "dwelling for G-d in the physical world" whose construction constitutes our mission in life. That's why the details are so important. But why do they have to be related twice? Couldn't the Torah simply say, "And the Children of Israel built it exactly as G-d had commanded"?

But the Torah wants to emphasize that there will always be two versions of G-d's home on earth: the ideal version, as G-d envisions it and describes it to Moses, and the real version, as it is actually built in and out of our physical lives.

Does this means that G-d is making allowances? That His vision can be compromised by "the way things are" down here? But *both versions are exactly the same* in the Torah's account! In other words, we are empowered-- and expected--to recreate the divine ideal in its entirety, down to every last peg, clasp and carrying pole, within the material world. Recreate--not duplicate. G-d does not want us to transform physical matter into substanceless spirit; He wants us to make the *physical* world hospitable to His presence.

Being human means never ceasing the effort to translate the ideal into the real. Not that we can eliminate the gap between matter and spirit. We can do better: we can make our lives a physical version of the divine vision. Human life is an attempt to achieve the impossible--an attempt that fails, and in failing, achieves something even greater.

If you're experiencing stress, you're doing something right.

Based on the teachings of the Rebbe
Reprinted with permission from chabad.org

Home

by **Rabbi Yanki Tauber**

Nations go to war over it, families sign away a sizeable chunk of their income for the next 30 years to acquire one. The sages of the Talmud go so far as to say that "A man without a homestead is not a man."

A home is more than a roof to keep out the rain, walls to keep out unwanted visitors, a kitchen in which to prepare food and a bed in which to sleep. Forts, office buildings, hotels and restaurants can perform those functions as well, or better, than any residence. But only at home is a person at home. Home is where you can make faces at the mirror, wear an old green sweater with a hole under the armpit and eat pickles with peanut butter—because you feel like it.

G-d, too, desires a home—a place where He can be fully and uninhibitedly Himself. The Chassidic masters ask: Why did G-d create the physical world? What can our coarse, finite, strife-ridden existence give Him that the spiritual dimensions of creation cannot? And they answer: G-d created the physical world because He wanted a home—a place where He can do things because He feels like it.

G-d's first home was a two-room, 45 by 15-foot building. According to Exodus 25, it was made of the following materials: gold; silver; copper; blue, purple and red-dyed wool; flax; goat hair; animal hides and wood. It was made to order, from detailed specifications given to Moses at Mount Sinai. It sat in the very center of the Israelite camp in the desert, and was designed so that it could be dismantled and reassembled as they wandered from place to place for the forty years between their Exodus from Egypt and their entry into the Holy Land. Later, a larger and more permanent version was constructed on the Temple Mount in Jerusalem.

Said G-d to man: I created wisdom, knowledge and understanding, and in these creations My mind dwells. I created love, justice and compassion, and in these my character resides. I created beauty, splendor and majesty, and in these I invest My personality. But none of these are My home, any more than the office at which you work or the theater at which you are entertained is yours. So I created physical matter—the most undivine thing I could conceive of—so that I should have a place in which there are no roles for Me to play and no characteristics for Me to project. Only My will to fulfill.

When you take your gold (your material excesses), your silver (your stolid middle-class wealth) and your copper (your pauper's subsistence pennies) and use them to fashion a reality that conforms to My will, you have made Me at home in My world no "below." G-d could very well reveal himself and in so doing remove all of the masks and garments in which he conceals Himself, thus eliminating the possibility of "worlds" and certainly of a world such as ours, which is seemingly totally independent of Him. If what the Midrash says is correct, what G-d demands is impossible, or at the very least exceedingly abnormal.

This seemingly insoluble paradox is appreciated by the philosophers and theologians of all nationalities and religions. There are clearly two very different realities—G-d and the world. Worldliness and G-dliness are irreconcilable and, therefore, one can attain one only at the expense of the other. Religious experience demands withdrawal from worldly life. In this sense, both the Catholic priest and the Buddhist monk are motivated by the same rationale. On the other hand, religious sensitivity is a definite drawback if one's aim in life is to rule Wall Street. In fact, a compromise can be hammered out. There can be times and places for pursuing Divinity, and other times and places for pursuing worldly ends. The proportion of time and effort spent in heavenly or in earthly pursuits is then determined by personal inclination. This is a philosophically sound approach that allows for a normal balanced life. The problem is that it is inconsistent with G-d's objective as propounded in the Midrash.

Contrary to all reason, the Jewish people have taken on the Divine task of converting this finite, physical world with all of its minutiae into a residence for G-d. If the conversion of a lump of iron into a car is abnormal and contrary to nature, how is one to view the conversion of a car into a vessel for revealing G-dliness? It is normal for a Scroll to reveal holiness just as it is for a car to reflect worldliness. For a car, or a house, or food to reveal G-dliness is unprecedented and totally beyond grasp. Nonetheless, this fusion of two mutually antithetical states of being into one reality is accomplished daily by Jews living Jewish lives.

How is it done? Simple. The directions are supplied in the Torah. The car is not driven on Shabbat, specifically because it is Shabbat. The house has *mezzuzahs* identifying it as a Jewish house and property of the Creator. The food is kosher and a *brachah* is recited before and after eating. The energy supplied by the food is used toward the service of G-d in learning Torah and performing mitzvot. The application of Torah and Mitzvot to each and every aspect of earthly existence transforms all worldly objects and affairs into vessels in which G-d's supernal will can be manifest. Thus, every mitzvah performed by every Jew produces another brick for G-d's residence.

The process has been slow and laborious. It is no accident that the word for Divine service, *avodah,* literally means work. Moreover, we have been engaged in this "work" for 3,300 years. There is little doubt, however, that the job is almost complete, and when it is, the G-dliness that is the life of all existence will be revealed in everything.

The Jew, then, cannot be normal. With his soul rooted in Divine will and his feet planted on the ground, he appears as an outsider in both heaven and earth. You want to be religious? Fine. Go sit in *shul* and study Torah. You want to be an active participant in modern worldly life? Also good. Find a lucrative, prestigious profession and get to work. But what has worldly life to do with G-d and G-d with worldly life? The answer, of course, is everything.

Based on the teachings of the Rebbe
Reprinted with permission from chabad.org

Lesson 6
Have a Heart

Introduction

Can you think your way to love? Can you change the way you feel? If you have come this far, you know it is possible.

In this final lesson, we show you how to use the power of your mind to nurture your emotions. This kind of focused contemplation is a powerful tool for personal transformation, and it is the key to lifelong spiritual growth.

Why Emotions?

Learning **Activity 1**

Take 30 seconds and try to think of something right now that will generate positive feelings, whether of being happy, calm, or loved.

Awe
A Contemplation on Awe

Text 1

ברם צריך להיות לזכרון תמיד ראשית העבודה ועיקרה ושרשה . . .
ולפחות צריך לעורר תחלה היראה הטבעית המסותרת בלב כל ישראל
שלא למרוד בממ״ה הקב״ה . . .
דהיינו להתבונן במחשבתו עכ״פ גדולת א״ס ב״ה ומלכותו
אשר היא מלכות כל עולמים עליונים ותחתונים
 . . . ומניח העליונים ותחתונים ומייחד מלכותו על עמו ישראל בכלל
ועליו בפרט כי חייב אדם לומר בשבילי נברא העולם
והוא גם הוא מקבל עליו מלכותו להיות מלך עליו
ולעבדו ולעשות רצונו בכל מיני עבודת עבד.
והנה ה׳ נצב עליו ומלא כל הארץ כבודו ומביט עליו
ובוחן כליות ולב אם עובדו כראוי.
ועל כן צריך לעבוד לפניו באימה וביראה כעומד לפני המלך

ne must, however, constantly bear in mind what is the beginning of the service of G-d as well as its core and root . . . .

One must first arouse the innate awe which lies hidden in the heart of every Jew not to rebel against the Supreme

King of Kings, the Holy One, blessed be He . . . .

This means that he should at least contemplate in his mind

the greatness of the blessed Infinite

and His kingship,

which extends to all worlds, both higher and lower . . .

yet He leaves aside [the creatures of] the higher worlds and [the creatures of] the lower worlds and uniquely bestows His kingship

upon His people Israel in general

and upon him in particular

for each person is obliged to say: "For my sake was the world created,"

and he for his part accepts His kingship upon himself, that He be king over him,

to serve Him and do His will in all kinds of work of service.

"And, behold, G-d Himself stands over him,"

[yet at the same time,] "The whole world is full with His Glory,"

and He scrutinizes him and searches his inner parts and his heart

[to see] if he is serving Him as is fitting.

Therefore, he must serve in His presence with awe like one standing before the king.

TANYA, CHAPTER 41

Learning Activity 2

Contemplation on Awe	Worksheet
the greatness of the blessed Infinite	
and His kingship,	
which extends to all worlds, both higher and lower,	
yet He leaves aside [the creatures of] the higher worlds and [the creatures of] the lower worlds and uniquely bestows His kingship	
upon His people Israel in general	
and upon him in particular,	
for each person is obliged to say: "For my sake was the world created."	
and he for his part accepts His kingship upon himself, that He be king over him,	
to serve Him and do His will in all kinds of work of service.	

Contemplation on Awe Worksheet

"And, behold, G-d Himself stands over him,"	
[yet at the same time] "The whole world is full with His Glory,"	
and He scrutinizes him and searches his inner parts and his heart	
to see if he is serving Him as is fitting.	

Text 2

עכ״פ כמורא בשר ודם הדיוט לפחות שאינו מלך המביט עליו
שנמנע בעבורו מלעשות דבר שאינו הגון בעיניו
שזו נקרא יראה כמו שאמר רבן יוחנן בן זכאי לתלמידיו
יהי רצון שיהא מורא שמים עליכם כמורא בשר ודם . . .
תדעו כשאדם עובר עבירה אומר שלא יראני אדם . . .
רק שיראה זו נקראת יראה תתאה ויראת חטא

One's awe of G-d should be at least like one's awe in the presence of an ordinary mortal, who is watching him . . . he would refrain from doing anything unseemly in the other's eyes. [Even] this is termed awe; as Rabban Yochanan ben Zakkai said to his disciples: "May it be G-d's will that the awe of heaven be upon you like the awe of a human being . . . . For you know that when a person commits a sin, he says to himself: 'May no one see me!' . . . ." Such awe, however, is termed as only "lower-level awe" and "fear of sin."

TANYA, CHAPTER 41

Text 3

וְהִיא הַיִּרְאָה הַטִּבְעִית הַמְסֻתֶּרֶת הַנַּ"ל
רַק שֶׁכְּדֵי שֶׁתָּבֹא לִידֵי מַעֲשֶׂה בִּבְחִי' יִרְאַת חֵטְא
לִהְיוֹת סוּר מֵרָע בְּמַעֲשֶׂה דִבּוּר וּמַחֲשָׁבָה
צָרִיךְ לְגַלּוֹתָהּ מִמִּצְפוּנֵי בִינַת הַלֵּב . . .
לְהָבִיאָהּ לִבְחִי' מַחֲשָׁבָה מַמָּשׁ שֶׁבַּמּוֹחַ
לְהַעֲמִיק בָּהּ מַחֲשַׁבְתּוֹ מֶשֶׁךְ זְמַן מָה מַמָּשׁ
עַד שֶׁתֵּצֵא פְּעֻלָּתָהּ מֵהַכֹּחַ אֶל הַפּוֹעַל מַמָּשׁ
דְּהַיְינוּ לִהְיוֹת סוּר מֵרָע וַעֲשֵׂה טוֹב בְּמַחֲשָׁבָה דִבּוּר וּמַעֲשֶׂה
מִפְּנֵי ה' הַצּוֹפֶה וּמַבִּיט וּמַאֲזִין וּמַקְשִׁיב וּמֵבִין אֶל כָּל מַעֲשֵׂהוּ וּבוֹחֵן כְּלָיוֹתָיו וְלִבּוֹ
וּכְמַאֲמַר רַזַ"ל הִסְתַּכֵּל בִּשְׁלֹשָׁה דְבָרִים כוּ' עַיִן רוֹאָה וְאֹזֶן שׁוֹמַעַת . . .
וְגַם כִּי אֵין לוֹ דְּמוּת הַגּוּף
הֲרֵי אַדְּרַבָּה הַכֹּל גָּלוּי וְיָדוּעַ לְפָנָיו בְּיֶתֶר שְׂאֵת לְאֵין קֵץ
מְרָאִית הָעַיִן וּשְׁמִיעַת הָאֹזֶן עַד"מ

And this is the natural, hidden awe referred to earlier.

However, in order that it should be translated into action in the sense of "fear of sin" so that one will turn away from evil in action, word, and thought, one needs to bring it to light from the hidden depths of the understanding of the heart . . . and to place it within the realm of actual [i.e., conscious] thought that is in the brain.

[This means] immersing his thought in it for a lengthy period of time until its effect will emerge from the potential into the actual, so that he will turn away from evil and do good in thought, speech, and action because of G-d who looks and sees, hears and listens, and perceives all his deeds and searches his "inner parts and heart."

As the Rabbis, of blessed memory, said: "Reflect upon three things [and you will not come to sin: Know what is above you]—an Eye that sees, and an Ear that hears (Avot II:1) . . . ." And although He has no bodily likeness, on the contrary, [that is the very reason that] everything is revealed and known to Him infinitely more than, for example, through the physical media of sight and hearing.

TANYA, CHAPTER 42

Text 4

והנה כל אדם מישראל יהיה מי שיהיה
כשיתבונן בזה שעה גדולה בכל יום
איך שהקב"ה מלא ממש את העליונים ואת התחתונים
ואת השמים ואת הארץ ממש מלא כל הארץ כבודו ממש
וצופה ומביט ובוחן כליותיו ולבו
וכל מעשיו ודבוריו וכל צעדיו יספור
אזי תקבע בלבו היראה לכל היום כולו
כשיחזור ויתבונן בזה אפילו בהתבוננות קלה
בכל עת ובכל שעה יהיה סור מרע ועשה טוב במחשבה דבור ומעשה
שלא למרות ח"ו עיני כבודו אשר מלא כל הארץ
וכמאמר רבן יוחנן בן זכאי לתלמידיו כנ"ל
וז"ש הכתוב כי אם ליראה את ה' אלהיך ללכת בכל דרכיו
שהיא יראה המביאה לקיום מצותיו ית' בסור מרע ועשה טוב.
והיא יראה תתאה הנ"ל

Now, each individual Jew, whoever he may be, when he ponders upon this for a considerable time each day—how G-d is truly omnipresent in the higher and lower worlds; and the

actual heaven and earth is truly filled with His glory; and that He looks, seeks, and searches "his inner parts and his heart," and all his actions and words; and counts his every step—then awe will be implanted in his heart throughout the day.

Later, when he will again contemplate this, even with a superficial reflection at any time or moment, he will turn away from evil and do good, in thought, speech, and action, so as not to rebel, G-d forbid, in the sight of His glory whereof the whole world is filled.

This is in accord with the statement of Rabbi Yochanan ben Zakkai to his disciples, quoted above.

This, then, is the meaning of the verse: "[G-d demands of you] only to have awe of the L-rd your G-d, to walk in all His ways (Devarim/Deuteronomy 10:12)."

For this is the awe that leads to the fulfillment of G-d's commandments, turning away from evil and doing good.

TANYA, CHAPTER 42

One Method for Generating Love:
The King and the Pauper

Text 5

ויש דרך ישר לפני איש שוה לכל נפש וקרוב הדבר מאד מאד
לעורר ולהאיר אור האהבה התקועה ומסותרת בלבו. . .
והוא כאשר ישים אל לבו
מ״ש הכתו׳ כמים הפנים לפנים כן לב האדם אל האדם
פי׳ כמו שכדמות וצורת הפנים שהאדם מראה במים
כן נראה לו שם במים צורה צורה עצמה
בלב חבירו אליו ג״כ ככה ממש לב האדם הנאמן באהבתו לאיש אחר
הרי האהבה זו מעוררת אהבה
להיות אוהבים נאמנים זה לזה
בפרט כשרואה אהבת חבירו אליו.
והנה זהו טבע הנהוג במדת כל אדם אף אם שניהם שוים במעלה
ועל אחת כמה וכמה אם מלך גדול ורב מראה אהבתו הגדולה והעצומה
לאיש הדיוט ונבזה ושפל אנשים ומנוול המוטל באשפה
ויורד אליו ממקו׳ כבודו עם כל שריו יחדיו ומקימו ומרימו מאשפתו
ומכניסו להיכלו היכל המלך חדר לפנים מחדר
מקום שאין כל עבד ושר נכנס לשם ומתייחד עמו שם ביחוד וקירוב אמיתי
וחיבוק ונישוק ואתדבקות רוחא ברוחא בכל לב ונפש
עאכ״ו שתתעורר ממילא האהבה כפולה ומכופלת
בלב ההדיוט ושפל אנשים הזה אל נפש המלך
בהתקשרות הנפש ממש מלב ונפש מעומקא דלבא לאין קץ.
ואף אם לבו כלב האבן המס ימס והיה למים

There is yet another direct way equally applicable to every person to arouse and kindle the light of the love that is implanted and concealed in his heart....

That is to take to heart the meaning of the verse: "As water mirrors the face to the face, so does the heart of one person mirror the other (Proverbs 27:19)."

This means that as in the case of the likeness and features of the face which a person presents to the water, the identical face is reflected back from the water, so also the heart of a person who is loyal in affection for another. For this love awakens a loving response for him or her in the heart of the friend also, so that they come to love each other loyally . . . .

Such is the common nature in the character of every person even when they [the lover and beloved] are equal in status. How much more so if a great and mighty king displays his great and intense love for a commoner who is despised and lowly among men, a disgraceful creature cast on the dunghill.

Yet the king comes down to him from the place of his glory, together with all his retinue, and raises him and exalts him from his dunghill and brings him into his palace—the royal palace, in the innermost chamber, a place such as no servant nor lord ever enters, and there shares with him the closest companionship with embraces and kisses and attachment of "spirit to spirit," with their whole heart and soul.

How much more so will there be aroused automatically a doubled and redoubled love in the heart of this most common and humble individual for the king, with a true attachment of spirit, from heart and soul, from the infinite depths of his heart. Even if his heart be like a heart of stone, it will surely melt and become [like] water, and his soul will pour itself out like water, with soulful longing for the love of the king.

TANYA, CHAPTER 46

Oneness—Conclusion of *Tanya*
Oil, Wick, and Flame

Text 6

וז״ש הינוקא דנהורא עילאה דאדליק על רישיה
היא שכינתא אצטריך למשחא . . .
ואינון עובדין טבין הן תרי״ג מצות . . .
כדי לאחוז אור השכינה בפתילה היא נפש החיונית שבגוף הנקראת פתילה עד״מ
כי כמו שבנר הגשמי האור מאיר ע״י כליון ושריפת הפתילה הנהפכת לאש
כך אור השכינה שורה על נפש האלהית על ידי כליון נפש הבהמית
והתהפכותה מחשוכא לנהורא וממרירו למתקא בצדיקים
או לפחות ע״י כליון לבושיה שהן מחשבה דבור ומעשה
והתהפכותן מחשך הקליפות לאור ה׳ . . . בבינונים
כי ע״י התהפכות נפש הבהמית הבאה מקליפ׳ נוגה מחשוכא לנהורא
נעשה בחי׳ העלאת מ״ן להמשיך אור השכינה על נפשו האלהית . . .
ובזה יובן היטב מ״ש כי ה׳ אלהיך אש אוכלה הוא . . .

And [when the Zohar says] "The G-dly light that is kindled on [the Jew's] head, meaning G-d's Presence, requires oil [good deeds]," namely, the 613 commandments . . . . [It means that]

thereby the light of G-d's Presence can cling to the wick, i.e., the [animal] soul in the body, which is metaphorically called a "wick."

For just as in the case of a physical candle, the light shines by virtue of the consumption and burning of the wick turning to fire, so does the light of G-d's Presence rest on the G-dly soul as a result of the consumption of the animal soul and its transformation from darkness to light in the case of *tsadikim,* or at least through the consumption of its garments—thought, speech, and action—and their transformation from the darkness of the *kelipot* to Divine light . . . in the case of *beinonim.*

For as a result of the transformation of the animal soul, originating from *kelipat nogah,* from darkness to light there is . . . drawn down the light of G-d's Presence . . . . Thereby one may clearly understand the text, "For the L-rd Your G-d is a consuming fire (Devarim 4:24)."

TANYA, CHAPTER 53

Appendix
Higher-Level Awe

Text A

Concerning this *yirah tata'ah* (lower-level awe) which is [necessary] for the fulfillment of His commandments, in both areas of "Turn away from evil and do good," it was said, "If there is no awe, there is no wisdom (Avot III:17)."

TANYA, CHAPTER 43

Text B

As for *yirah ila'ah* (higher-level awe), an awe stemming from a sense of shame before G-d's greatness, and an inner sense of awe that derives from the inward aspects of G-dliness within the worlds, concerning this level of awe it was said by our Sages, "If there is no wisdom, there is no awe (Avot III:17)," and, "Who is wise? He who sees that which comes into being (Tamid 32a)." That is to say, he sees how everything is born and created from non-being to being by means of the Word of G-d and the breath of His mouth, as it is written, "And by the breath of His mouth all their hosts [were created] (Tehilim/Psalms 33:6)." Therefore, the heavens and the earth and all their hosts are truly nullified out of existence within the Word of G-d and the breath of His mouth and are accounted as nothing at all, as naught and nothingness indeed, just as the light and brightness of the sun are nullified within the body of the sun itself. And no man should except himself from this principle that also his body and soul are utterly nullified in the Word of G-d .... However, one cannot attain this awe and wisdom except by means of the fulfillment of the Torah and *mitzvot* through lower-level awe, which is an external awe. And this is what is meant by the statement, "If there is no awe, there is no wisdom."

TANYA, CHAPTER 43

Ahavah Rabah and *Ahavat Olam*

Text C

Now, in love too there are two grades—*ahavah rabah* and *ahavat olam*. *Ahavah rabah* is a love of delights and it is a fiery flame that rises of itself. It comes from Above by way of a gift to him who is already perfect in awe .... Without the prerequisite of awe, it is impossible to attain the level of *ahavah rabah*.

TANYA, CHAPTER 43

Ahavat olam, however, is that which comes from the understanding and knowledge of the greatness of G-d, the Infinite Who fills all worlds, and encompasses all worlds, and before Whom everything is accounted as nothing at all.

As a result of such contemplation, the attribute of love which is in the soul will automatically divest itself of its interests. That is, it will not clothe itself in any other pleasure or enjoyment whether physical or spiritual, to love it, and will not desire anything whatever in the world other than G-d alone, the Source of the vitality of all enjoyments. For they are all nullified in reality and are accounted as nothing at all, compared with Him, there being no manner of comparison or similarity between them, G-d forbid, just as there is no comparison between that which is absolutely naught and nothing—and everlasting life.

TANYA, CHAPTER 43

Key Points

1. Changing who we are means changing our emotional capacities.

2. There are two basic emotions and they are opposites: awe and love. We innately feel both towards G-d, but must work to both reveal and develop them.

3. Awe must come first, but both are necessary as are two wings to a bird.

4. Awe should inspire a person to carefully consider his actions.

5. Contemplating the greatness of G-d, i.e., "the whole world full with His glory," then deeply meditating on this verse, will naturally lead towards the cultivation of awe.

6. Love comes after respect: beyond respecting the other's limits, one must proactively and lovingly extend himself beyond personal limits for the sake of the recipient.

7. We can harness love through the principle of "emotional reciprocity" inasmuch as we contemplate how much G-d cares for us and does for us on a daily and even second-by-second basis.

8. The basic principle behind such contemplation is that intellectual contemplation gives rise to emotions, and the "mind rules over the heart."

9. The book of *Tanya* ends by giving meaning to our struggle, by reiterating our power to transform ourselves and the world. The book provides us with encouragement, to sustain us on our never-ending journey of continued growth.

Additional Readings

A Man I Met in Shul

by **Dr. Yaakov Brawer**
from the introduction to his book,
Something From Nothing (Tav, 1990)

One sunny Shabbat morning 20 years ago, I awoke to find myself standing in shul, enwrapped in a *tallit* with prayer book in hand. I hadn't actually arisen from sleep, but rather from an absorbing daydream in which I was speculating about the possible results of an experiment that I had planned for the following week. Although the experience was hardly novel, it crystallized and defined for me a religious crisis that had been lurking in my subconscious for some time.

How was it possible, on Shabbat, a day of transcendent holiness and limitless spiritual possibilities, to stand before one's Creator and to address Him in prayer without so much as a thought to what one is doing? If I were standing before--*l'havdil*--the Dean of Medicine, my mouth would be dry, my heart rate would be elevated and the rest of the world would disappear from my consciousness as if it didn't exist. How could I be so blasé about an encounter with the Almighty? Where was the awe and love? Where was the excitement? How was it possible to put on a *tallit* with no more deliberation than that required for putting on one's shirt? What was wrong with me?

Although advice was abundant, the problem remained. I was told that I was expecting too much and that I should be happy with what I had accomplished. I was advised to concentrate more deeply on talmudic learning, to not focus so much on talmudic learning, to take regular exercise and get more sleep, and to visit a cemetery so that I would learn to appreciate the great gift of life. I was told that the fervor for which I yearned no longer existed and one rabbinic friend even suggested that I was better off without intense feeling since emotion interferes with technical performance of the mitzvot. Apparently our relationship with G-d is expected to settle into a comfortable, if prosaic, routine defined as normative orthodox observance.

One Shabbat I walked into Shul and saw a chassid standing at the back. He had his *tallit* over his shoulder and was obviously preparing for prayer. I gave him little thought until three and a half hours later when I got ready to leave for home. The chassid was standing in the same place with his *tallit* still over his shoulder. He hadn't yet begun his prayers. His eyes were closed and his face burned with a spiritual intensity that I had never before seen. I was thrilled. I could not imagine what sort of contemplation brought him to such a state of spiritual awakening, but it clearly had nothing to do with cholent or kugel, which were my main preoccupations at noontime on Shabbat.

In this chassid, I had found half the answer to my problem. I now knew that fiery devotion in the service of G-d was, in fact, achievable, although I couldn't fathom how. Here was a man who knew before Whom he was standing. I took great comfort in surreptitiously watching my chassid, and for a while I was content with the simple knowledge that such a person existed. After observing him for a few weeks, I got up the nerve to go over and introduce myself.

I had no idea of what his response would be and I was more than a little uneasy. Before I could open my mouth, he put his hand on my shoulder and said, "I know what you want. You want to see the *koach hapoel b'hanifal* (roughly, 'the power of the Creator in Creation')." Before I could answer, he told me that he would come to my house on the following Thursday night and begin studying Chassidus with me. Thus began my 20-year love affair with Chassidic teaching.

Reprinted with permission from chabad.org

Climbing the Ladder

by **Rabbi Yanki Tauber**

Behold, a ladder stood on the earth, and the top of it reached to heaven; and behold, angels of G-dwere ascending and descending on it.
(Genesis 28:12)

What motivates you? Why do you do what you do?

Do you wake up in the morning, go to work, are considerate to your spouse, patient with your children and nice to your neighbors because you are forced to? Because society rewards such behavior? Because you want to? Because you can't imagine acting otherwise?

A close examination of our actions in the course of the day and the motivations that drive them would probably reveal elements of all of the above. But are these random influences, or is there some sort of order and hierarchy to them? And if there is, in what order are they aligned? And where is your life and psyche headed—is it advancing up the ladder or sliding down the stairwell?

According to the ancient mystics, all actions of man—indeed all workings of creation—derive from two general forces: love and awe. More specifically, there are two types of love: "lower love" and "higher love." And two forms of awe—"lower awe" and "higher awe."

"Lower awe" is the lowest of the four on the ladder of human motivations. A step above that is "lower love." Then comes "higher love." Finally, "higher awe" is the highest level a human being can reach.

[This hierarchy is alluded to in the verse, "And these are the chronicles of Isaac the son of Abraham; Abraham gave birth to Isaac" (Genesis 25:19). According to the Kabbalists, Abraham was the embodiment of the attribute of love, while Isaac embodied awe. The verse repeats itself, signifying that there is a lower and higher Abraham, as well as a lower and a higher Isaac. And the

order in which their names appear is: Isaac, Abraham, Abraham, Isaac; in other words—awe, love, love, awe.]

"Lower awe" is fear. When we keep our hands out of the cookie jar because we'll be punished if we're caught, when we follow the rules at work to avoid being fired and having our spouse yell at us and call us a good-for-nothing, when we obey G-d's laws out of fear of divine retribution in the afterlife—we're acting out of fear. We're operating on the lowest rung of human virtue—lower awe (which is still a whole lot higher than human iniquity).

A step above that is "lower love"—the impulse to do something because we receive something positive in return. Every day, we do countless things—including things that require a great degree of effort and toil—because these things bring us physical pleasure, emotional joy, intellectual stimulation, peace of mind or spiritual fulfillment. Yes, we're acting "selfishly", but we're also giving of ourselves, willingly and freely rather than compulsively, and often we're giving up something immediate and tangible for the sake of something more ethereal. On the whole, it's a self-expanding experience, rather than the self-constricting fear of "lower awe".

"Higher love" is altruistic love—when we give of ourselves out of a pure desire to give. For while it is true that we are driven by a core impulse for self-preservation and self-enhancement, we also possess a higher self, a soul that is "a spark of G-dliness" whose core desire is to give rather than take, to serve rather than receive. Whenever we find ourselves motivated to pursue truth simply because it is true, to do goodness for no reason other than that it is good, that is our G-dly self asserting itself over our selfish self, a flash of our divine spark peeking through the veil of "lower love" that dominates so much of our psyche and personality.

But there is something that is even higher than "higher love". Higher love is when we do something because we want to; "higher awe" is when we do something because we are in touch with something greater than ourselves and our desires. Watch a *tzaddik* praying to G-d, a soldier sacrificing his very life to protect his people, a parent interacting with her child. There is something here that's beyond selfishness or selflessness—beyond the self and its need to receive or to give. It is something that occurs when the self is awed by something that is infinitely greater than itself, and submits to it not because it is forced to, or enticed to, or even wants to, but because its finite self has become part of the Infinite.

The endeavor of what we call "life" is to ascend this ladder, to climb these four rungs of transcendence. Climbing the ladder doesn't mean that we'll attain a state in which everything we do is on the highest of the four planes; nor does it mean that we'll leave the lower levels behind us as we ascend to the ones above it: there will always be things that we do out of fear, out of love of self, out of altruistic desire, and out of sublime awe. Ascending the ladder means being aware of these four levels, aware of their relationship vis-a-vis each other, knowing which way is up and which way is down, and always striving upwards.

Based on the teachings of the Rebbe
Reprinted with permission from chabad.org

Do We Love Too Much?

by **Rabbi Yanki Tauber**

short/ cir-cuit/ (elect.): an abnormal, usually unintentional condition of relatively low resistance between two points of different potential in a circuit, usually resulting in a flow of excess current.
Random House Dictionary of the English Language

Do we love too much?

Apparently we do. Many marriages fail for a dearth of love; an equal number are suffocated by an overabundance of the same.

So desirous are we for connection, so hungry for communion with another human being, that we forget that for love to endure it must be complemented with an equal measure of restraint. So eager are we to give of ourselves to the one we love—be it a spouse, a child, or a friend—that we often give without consideration of the needs and desires of the recipient of our love.

When passion is mitigated with a degree of inhibition, when intimacy is tempered with a modicum of reserve, love flourishes. But when all limits are betrayed, love burns out.

A love relationship can thus be compared to an electrical circuit. In a circuit, the attraction between the positive and negative charges creates a current of energy joining the two; the current meets with a certain degree of resistance as it passes through the circuit, delimiting its intensity. The natural tendency of this attraction is to seek the shortest possible route, carrying the highest possible current, to join the attracted charges. But should this tendency be indulged—should the "resistance" fall—the circuit will "short": the current will escalate, ultimately causing the destruction of the circuit and the breakdown of the very connection which the current seeks to create.

The Book of Leviticus speaks of the tragic death of Aaron's two elder sons, Nadav and Avihu.

After many months of labor and anticipation, the Sanctuary had finally been set up in the Israelite camp and the Divine Presence came to rest within it. Amidst the joyous dedication ceremonies, "Nadav and Avihu each took his censer, and put fire in it, and put *ketoret* (incense) on it, and offered strange fire before G-d, which He commanded them not. And a fire went out from G-d, and consumed them, and they died before G-d (Leviticus 10:1-2)."

In his commentary on Torah, the great sage and mystic Rabbi Chaim ibn Atar explains that Nadav and Avihu died from an overdose of love.

Once a year, on Yom Kippur, the High Priest would enter the innermost chamber of the Sanctuary, the Holy of Holies, to offer *ketoret* to G-d. This occasion—on which the most spiritual human being performed the most sacred service in the holiest place in the world on the holiest day of the year—was the point of utmost intimacy with G-d attained by man. Nadav and Avihu were priests, but not High Priests (though they would have been, had they lived to succeed their father in that office); it was a very special occasion, marked by special offerings to G-d, but it was not Yom Kippur. But their thirst for intimacy with G-d could not be satisfied by anything less than the ultimate. They wanted to get closer yet, though, "He commanded them not."

Human life is a love affair between the soul and her G-d. Our passion for life is a craving for the "spark of G-dliness" implicit within every one of G-d's creations; ultimately, everything we do is motivated by our soul's desire to draw closer to our Source. So powerful is this desire, that it can lead us to do things that are contrary to G-d's will—things that violate the bounds of our love and destroy it.

For our marriage to live and thrive, we must feed our passion for life; but we must also know when to hold back. As in every truly loving relationship, we must learn to love in the manner that our beloved needs and desires to be loved.

Based on the teachings of the Rebbe
Reprinted with permission from chabad.org

How Can One Love an Unknowable G-d?

by **Rabbi Tzvi Freeman**

Question:

We're told that G-d is unknowable, but also told to love G-d. I don't get it: how can one love something that is "Unknowable"?

Answer:

Many men will tell you that after 25 years of marriage the woman they have lived with is still a great mystery to them. As my father-in-law put it in his typical engineer terminology, "By now, I have figured out which buttons to push. But I still have no idea how she works."

And yes, my father-in-law was madly in love with his wife after over 30 years at the time he said this.

What I'm getting at is that the same applies with G-d. Yes, He is entirely unknowable—because He has no definition. But we do know how He relates to us, what He has created, and which buttons to press.

So that's where love comes in: We see that this infinite, unknowable G-d—who has created a magnificent universe with endless stars and galaxies and even more creatures of unbelievable diversity, including us tiny creatures—actually desires a relationship with us. And He gives us the tools to build that relationship, a relationship so close and intimate that we can be with Him every moment of our day, in soul, mind and every limb of our body. If we would really think deeply into this, no doubt our hearts would melt.

(Rabbi Schneur Zalman of Liadi expands on this idea in chapter 46 of his *Tanya*.)

Reprinted with permission from chabad.org

Acknowledgments

irst and foremost, above all, thanks and praise are due to the Almighty G-d, who has given us life, and whose abundant kindness has sustained us until this day, and who has given us our teacher, the Rebbe, of blessed memory, as a guide for our generation.

This course on *Tanya* has been a long time in the making, starting with the *Map of Tanya* which I first drafted five years ago. Thanks must go to **Rabbi Yosef B. Friedman**, of the Kehot Publication Society who picked up the project in its infancy, as well as to **Rabbi Dovid Olidort**, of the Kehot Publication Society, who helped prepare the final draft of the map, as well as collaborating to create a fitting Hebrew translation. I must also acknowledge **Spotlight Design**, who took on the challenge of giving the map its unique look.

Two years ago, when I was approached by the **Rohr Jewish Learning Institute** to turn the map into a course, it was **Mrs. Chana Silberstein** who helped me hash out the initial concept for the course. Mrs. Silberstein has been there every step of the way, from brainstorming new ideas to editing what I thought were final drafts. Her dedication and expertise have been no less than astounding.

The **JLI** editorial board was of invaluable assistance in adapting my work on *Tanya* to the **JLI** format. Thank you, **Rabbi Hesh Epstein, Rabbi Shmuel Kaplan, Rabbi Benny Rapoport, Rabbi Yisrael Rice,** and **Rabbi Avrohom Sternberg**.

Rabbi Berel Bell was instrumental in helping shape the course from its earliest to its final stages. Thank you, Rabbi Bell, for teaching me (and reminding me repeatedly) that, "It's not what you tell the students that counts, but what they are going to come away with after class."

Thanks go to **Mrs. Michla Schanowitz**, who provided notes on an early draft which gave much of the impetus for a reworking of the course, and who also provided transcripts from the recordings of Rabbi Manis Friedman.

I'd like to give a special thanks to **Rabbi Sholom Raichik**, who piloted the course and gave me tremendous insight as to how the words I had written would actually play out in the field. In addition, Rabbi Raichik' pointed out many rough transitions and forced me to articulate the lessons more clearly.

Thanks to **Rabbi Manis Friedman** for listening to all of my ideas about this course and about *Chasidut* in general. I am extremely grateful for Rabbi Friedman's ongoing encouragement and mentorship.

I must also acknowledge **Rabbi Yisroel Shmotkin**, head *shliach* to the state of Wisconsin, who made it possible for me to devote time to this project. Rabbi Shmotkin has been an indispensible resource of information and guidance for me, and his leadership has been an inspiration.

The staff at **JLI Central** has helped bring this project to fruition. Thanks are due to our copyeditor, **Mrs. Ya'akovah Weber**; Nachman Levine, for layout and design; and **Shimon Leib Jacobs**, for printing.

It has been a privilege to author this course for the **Rohr Jewish Learning Institute**. For this opportunity, my thanks to **Rabbi Efraim Mintz**, JLI's executive director, as well as **JLI's** principal patron, **Rabbi Moshe Kotlarsky**, and JLI's primary benefactors, **George** and **Pamela Rohr**.

Special thanks to **chabad.org**, an invaluable online resource of Jewish learning and information, for providing many of the articles for our Additional Readings.

Finally, thanks to **B.T.**, who has been there through this whole process.

Rabbi Shais Taub

Milwaukee, Wisconsin

Elul, 5768

The Rohr Jewish Learning Institute

An affiliate of
Merkos L'Inyonei Chinuch
The Educational Arm of
The Chabad Lubavitch Movement
822 Eastern Parkway, Brooklyn, NY 11213

Marketing Committee
Rabbi Mendy Halberstam
Coordinator

Rabbi Yehuda Shemtov
Rabbi Simcha Backman
Rabbi Ronnie Fine
Rabbi Ovadiah Goldman

Marketing Consultants
Gary Wexler
Passion Marketing

Tzvi Freeman

J.J. Gross
Blowdart Advertising & Marketing

Alan Rosenspan

Alan M. Shafer
Alliant Marketing Solutions

Warren Modlin
MednetPro, Inc.

Online Division
Rabbi Mendel Bell
Rabbi Mendel Sirota

Administration
Rabbi Yoni Katz
Rabbi Mendel Sirota
Rabbi Mendy Weg

Affiliate Support
Rabbi Shmuli Wolvovsky
Rabbi Mendel Sirota

Affiliate Liaisons
Rivka Sternberg
Nechama Shmotkin
Mindy Wallach
Shaina Fine

Publication Design
Nachman Levine

Research Editor
Nachman Levine

Copy Editor
Ya'akovah Weber

Graphic Design
Gershon Eichorn
Zalman Stock
Yitzchok Goldberg
Spotlight Design

Accounting
Nechama Shmotkin
Shaina B. Mintz

Printing
Shimon Leib Jacobs
Point One Communications

Multimedia Development
Rabbi Levi Brod
Rabbi Benny Rapoport
Rabbi Chesky Edelman
Rabbi Levi Teldon
Rabbi Dr. Shmuel Klatzkin

JLI Departments

Torah Studies
Rabbi Yossi Gansburg
Chairman
Toronto, ON

Rabbi Meir Hecht
Director

Rabbi Yechezkel Deitsch
Mrs. Nechama Shmotkin
Administrators

Sinai Scholars Society
in partnership with
Chabad on Campus

Rabbi Menachem Schmidt
Chairman
Philadelphia, PA

Rabbi Moshe Chaim Dubrowski
Chabad on Campus

Rabbi Yitzchok Dubov
Director

Rabbi Lev Cotlar
Affiliate Liaison

myShiur:
Advanced Learning Initiative
Rabbi Shmuel Kaplan
Chairman
Baltimore, MD

Rabbi Levi Kaplan
Director

National Jewish Retreat
Rabbi Hesh Epstein
Chairman
Columbia, SC

Rabbi Yoni Katz
Director

Rabbi Mendy Weg
Coordinator

Bruce Backman
Liaison

Advisory Board
Annette Batkin
Stephen Batkin
Sonia Beker
Eileen Bruskewitz
Rabbi Chaim Drizin
Dr. Barbara Grossman
Dr. Michael Grossman
Dr. Peter Pflaum
Dr. Stephen Serbin
Steven Lehat

JLI Teacher Training
Rabbi Berel Bell
Director

JLI For Teens
Rabbi Chaim Block
Chairman

Rabbi Benny Rapoport
Director

JLI International Desk
Rabbi Moshe Heber
Coordinator

Torah Café Online Learning
Rabbi Levi Kaplan
Director

Department of Continuing Professional Education
Dr. Chana Silberstein
Chair, Curriculum and Development

Dr. Michael Akerman, MD
Consultant for Continuing
Medical Education
Associate Professor of Medicine,
SUNY-Downstate Medical Center

Mrs. Mindy Wallach
Administrator
Continuing Medical Education

Bernard Kanstoroom, Esq.
Consultant for Continuing
Legal Education Events
Bethesda, Maryland

Mrs. Rivka Sternberg
Mrs. Shaina Fine
Administrators
Continuing Legal Education

Rohr JLI Affiliates

Share the **Rohr JLI** experience with friends and relatives worldwide

ALABAMA
BIRMINGHAM
Rabbi Yossi Friedman
205.970.0100

ARIZONA
CHANDLER
Rabbi Mendel Deitsch
480.855.4333

GLENDALE
Rabbi Sholom Lew
602.375.2422

PHOENIX
Rabbi Zalman Levertov
Rabbi Yossi Friedman
602.944.2753

SCOTTSDALE
Rabbi Yossi Levertov
Rabbi Yossi Bryski
480.998. 1410

CALIFORNIA
AGOURA HILLS
Rabbi Moshe Bryski
Rabbi Yisroel Levin
Rabbi Shlomo Bistritzky
818.991.0991

BAKERSFIELD
Rabbi Shmuel Schlanger
661.835.8381

BEL AIR
Rabbi Chaim Mentz
310.475.5311

BRENTWOOD
Rabbi Boruch Hecht
Rabbi Mordechai Zaetz
310.826.4453

BURBANK
Rabbi Shmuly Kornfeld
818.954.0070

CALABASAS
Rabbi Eliyahu Friedman
818.585.1888

CARLSBAD
Rabbi Yeruchem Eilfort
Rabbi Michoel Shapiro
760.943.8891

CHATSWORTH
Rabbi Yossi Spritzer
818.718.0777

CUPERTINO
Rabbi Reuven Goldstein
408.725.0910

GLENDALE
Rabbi Simcha Backman
818.240.2750

HUNTINGTON BEACH
Rabbi Aron Berkowitz
714.846.2285

IRVINE
Rabbi Alter Tenenbaum
Rabbi Elly Andrusier
949.786.5000

LAGUNA BEACH
Rabbi Elimelech Gurevitch
949 499 0770

LOMITA
Rabbi Eli Hecht
Rabbi Sholom Pinson
310.326.8234

LONG BEACH
Rabbi Abba Perelmuter
562.621.9828

LOS FELIZ
Rabbi Leibel Korf
323.660.5177

MALIBU
Rabbi Levi Cunin
310.456.6588

MARINA DEL REY
Rabbi Danny Yiftach
Rabbi Mendy Avtzon
310.859.0770

MILL VALLEY
Rabbi Hillel Scop
415.381.3794

MISSION VIEJO
Rabbi Zalman Aron Kantor
949.770.1270

MONTEREY
Rabbi Dovid Holtzberg
831.643.2770

MT. OLYMPUS
Rabbi Sholom Ber Rodal
323-650-1444

NAPA
Rabbi Elchonon Tenenbaum
707.320.2348

NEWHALL
Rabbi Elchonon Marosov
661.254.3434

NEWPORT BEACH
Rabbi Reuven Mintz
949.721.9800

NORTH HOLLYWOOD
Rabbi Nachman Abend
818.989.9539

NORTHRIDGE
Rabbi Eli Rivkin
818.368.3937

PACIFIC PALISADES
Rabbi Zushe Cunin
310.454.7783

PASADENA
Rabbi Chaim Hanoka
626.564.8820

RANCHO CUCAMONGA
Rabbi Sholom B. Harlig
909.949.4553

RANCHO PALOS VERDES
Rabbi Yitzchok Magalnic
310.544.5544

REDONDO BEACH
Rabbi Dovid Lisbon
310.214.4999

ROSEVILLE
Rabbi Yossi Korik
916.677.9960

SACRAMENTO
Rabbi Mendy Cohen
916.455.1400

S. BARBARA
Rabbi Yosef Loschak
805.683.1544

S. CLEMENTE
Rabbi Menachem M. Slavin
949.489.0723

S. CRUZ
Rabbi Yochanan Friedman
831.454.0101

S. DIEGO
Rabbi Motte Fradkin
858.547.0076

S. FRANCISCO
Rabbi Peretz Mochkin
415.571.8770

S. JOSE
Rabbi Aaron Cunin
408.358.5530

S. MATEO
Rabbi Yosef Marcus
650.341.4510

S. MONICA
Rabbi Boruch Rabinowitz
310.394.5699

S. Rafael
Rabbi Yisrael Rice
415.492.1666

S. Rosa
Rabbi Mendel Wolvovsky
707.577.0277

Simi Valley
Rabbi Nosson Gurary
805.577.0573

Stockton
Rabbi Avremel Brod
209.952.2081

Studio City
Rabbi Yossi Baitelman
818.508.6633

Temecula
Rabbi Yitzchok Hurwitz
951.303.9576

Thousand Oaks
Rabbi Chaim Bryski
805.493.7776

Tustin
Rabbi Yehoshua Eliezrie
714.508.2150

Ventura
Rabbi Yakov Latowicz
Mrs. Sarah Latowicz
805.658.7441

West Hills
Rabbi Avrahom Yitzchak Rabin
818.337.4544

Yorba Linda
Rabbi Dovid Eliezrie
714.693.0770

COLORADO
Aspen
Rabbi Mendel Mintz
970.544.3770

Boulder
Rabbi Pesach Scheiner
303.494.1638

Colorado Springs
Rabbi Moshe Liberow
719.634.2345

Denver
Rabbi Yossi Serebryanski
303.744.9699

Highlands Ranch
Rabbi Avraham Mintz
303.694.9119

Vail
Rabbi Dovid Mintz
970.476.7887

Westminster
Rabbi Benjy Brackman
303.429.5177

CONNECTICUT
Branford
Rabbi Yossi Yaffe
203.488.2263

Glastonbury
Rabbi Yosef Wolvovsky
860.659.2422

Greenwich
Rabbi Yossi Deren
Rabbi Menachem Feldman
203.629.9059

Litchfield
Rabbi Yoseph Eisenbach
860.567.3609

New London
Rabbi Avrohom Sternberg
860.437.8000

Orange
Rabbi Sheya Hecht
Rabbi Adam Haston
203.795.5261

Ridgefield
Rabbi Sholom Y. Deitsch
203.748.4421

Stamford
Rabbi Yisrael Deren
Rabbi Levi Mendelow
203.3.CHABAD

Westport
Rabbi Yehuda L. Kantor
Mrs. Dina Kantor
203.226.8584

West Hartford
Rabbi Yosef Gopin
Rabbi Shaya Gopin
860.659.2422

DELAWARE
Wilmington
Rabbi Chuni Vogel
302.529.9900

FLORIDA
Aventura
Rabbi Laivi Forta
Rabbi Chaim I. Drizin
305.933.0770

Bal Harbour
Rabbi Mendy Levy
305.868.1411

Boca Raton
Rabbi Moishe Denberg
Rabbi Zalman Bukiet
561.417.7797

East Boca Raton
Rabbi Ruvi New
561.417.7797

Bonita Springs
Rabbi Mendy Greenberg
239.949.6900

Boynton Beach
Rabbi Yosef Yitzchok Raichik
561.732.4633

Bradenton
Rabbi Menachem Bukiet
941.388.9656

Brandon
Rabbi Mendel Rubashkin
813.657.9393

Coconut Creek
Rabbi Yossi Gansburg
954.422.1987

Coral Gables
Rabbi Avrohom Stolik
305.490.7572

Deerfield Beach
Rabbi Yossi Goldblatt
954 422 1735

Fort Lauderdale
Rabbi Yitzchok Naparstek
954.568.1190

Fort Myers
Rabbi Yitzchok Minkowicz
Mrs. Nechama Minkowicz
239.433.7708

Hollywood
Rabbi Leizer Barash
954.965.9933

Rabbi Yossi Korf
Rabbi Yakov Garfinkel
954.967.8341

Kendall
Rabbi Yossi Harlig
305.234.5654

Key Biscayne
Rabbi Yoel Caroline
305.365.6744

Key West
Rabbi Yaakov Zucker
305.295.0013

Miami Beach
Rabbi Zev Katz
305.672.6613

Miami Downtown
Rabbi Chaim Lipskar
786.368.9040

Naples
Rabbi Fishel Zaklos
239.262.4474

North Miami Beach
Rabbi Moishe Kievman
305.770.1919

Orlando
Rabbi Yosef Konikov
407.354.3660

Parkland
Rabbi Mendy Gutnik
954.796.7330

S. Petersburg
Rabbi Alter Korf
727.344.4900

Sarasota
Rabbi Chaim Shaul Steinmetz
941.925.0770

Sunny Isles Beach
Rabbi Yisrael Baron
Classes in English
305.792.4770

Sunny Isles Beach
Rabbi Alexander Kaller
Classes in Russian
305.803.5315

Tallahassee
Rabbi Schneur Zalmen Oirechman
850.523.9294

Venice
Rabbi Sholom Ber Schmerling
941.493.2770

Weston
Rabbi Yisroel Spalter
Rabbi Yechezkel Unsdorfer
954.349.6565

West Palm Beach
Rabbi Yoel Gancz
561.659.7770

GEORGIA
Alpharetta
Rabbi Hirshy Minkowicz
770.410.9000

Atlanta
Rabbi Yossi New
Rabbi Isser New
404.843.2464

Atlanta: Intown
Rabbi Eliyahu Schusterman
Rabbi Ari Sollish
404.898.0434

Gwinnett
Rabbi Yossi Lerman
678.595.0196

Marietta
Rabbi Ephraim Silverman
Rabbi Zalman Charytan
770.565.4412

IDAHO
Boise
Rabbi Mendel Lifshitz
208.853.9200

ILLINOIS
Chicago
Rabbi Boruch Hertz
773.743.5434

Rabbi Meir Hecht
312.714.4655

Glenview
Rabbi Yishaya Benjaminson
847.998.9896

Highland Park
Mrs. Michla Schanowitz
847.266.0770

Northbrook
Rabbi Meir Moscowitz
847.564.8770

Peoria
Rabbi Eli Langsam
309.692.2250

Skokie
Rabbi Yochanan Posner
847.677.1770

Wilmette
Rabbi Dovid Flinkenstein
847.251.7707

INDIANA
Indianapolis
Rabbi Mendel Schusterman
317.251.5573

KANSAS
Overland Park
Rabbi Mendy Wineberg
913.649.4852

LOUISIANA
Metairie
Rabbi Yossi Nemes
504.454.2910

MARYLAND
Bethesda
Rabbi Bentzion Geisinsky
Rabbi Sender Geisinsky
301.913.9777

Baltimore
Rabbi Elchonon Lisbon
410.358.4787

Rabbi Velvel Belinsky
Classes in Russian
410.764.5000

Baltimore Downtown
Rabbi Levi Druk
410.605.0505

Columbia
Rabbi Hillel Baron
410.740.2424

Gaithersburg
Rabbi Sholom Raichik
301.926.3632

Potomac
Rabbi Mendel Bluming
301.983.4200

Silver Spring
Rabbi Berel Wolovsky
301.593.1117

MASSACHUSETTS
The Berkshires
Rabbi Levi Volovik
413.499.9899

Brighton
Rabbi Dan Rodkin
Rabbi Shmuel Bronstein
617.787.2200

Chestnut Hill
Rabbi Mendy Uminer
617.738.9770

Hyannis
Rabbi Yekusiel Alperowitz
508.775.2324

Longmeadow
Rabbi Yakov Wolff
413.567.8665

Natick
Rabbi Levi Fogelman
508.650.1499

Sharon
Rabbi Chaim Wolosow
Rabbi Ilan Meyers
781.784.4269

Sudbury
Rabbi Yisroel Freeman
978.443.3691

Swampscott
Mrs. Layah Lipsker
781.581.3833

Quincy
Rabbi Samuel Bronstein
617.850.5935

MICHIGAN
Ann Arbor
Rabbi Aharon Goldstein
734.995.3276

West Bloomfield
Rabbi Kasriel Shemtov
248.788.4000
Rabbi Elimelech Silberberg
Rabbi Avrohom Wineberg
248.855 .6170

MINNESOTA
Minnetonka
Rabbi Mordechai Grossbaum
952.929.9922

MISSOURI
S. Louis
Rabbi Yosef Landa
314.725.0400

NEVADA
Las Vegas
Rabbi Shea Harlig
Rabbi Tzvi Bronstein
702.259.0770

SUMMERLIN
Rabbi Yisroel Schanowitz
Rabbi Tzvi Bronstein
702.855.0770

NEW JERSEY
BASKING RIDGE
Rabbi Mendy Herson
908.604.8844

CHERRY HILL
Rabbi Mendy Mangel
856.874.1500

CLINTON
Rabbi Eli Kornfeld
908.623.7000

FORT LEE
Rabbi Meir Konikov
201.886.1238

FRANKLIN LAKES
Rabbi Chanoch Kaplan
201.848.0449

HILLSBOROUGH
Rabbi Shmaya Krinsky
908.874.0444

HOBOKEN
Rabbi Moshe Shapiro
201.386.5222

MADISON
Rabbi Shalom Lubin
973.377.0707

MANALAPAN
Rabbi Boruch Chazanow
732.972.3687

MARGATE
Rabbi Avrohom Rapoport
609.822.8500

MEDFORD
Rabbi Yitzchok Kahan
609.953.3150

NORTH BRUNSWICK
Rabbi Levi Azimov
732.398.9492

RANDOLPH
Rabbi Avraham Bechor
973.895.3070

ROCKAWAY
Rabbi Asher Herson
Rabbi Mordechai Baumgarten
973.625.1525

TEANECK
Rabbi Ephraim Simon
201.907.0686

TENAFLY
Rabbi Mordechai Shain
Rabbi Chaim Boyarsky
201.871.1152

TOMS RIVER
Rabbi Moshe Gourarie
732.349.4199

WAYNE
Rabbi Michel Gurkov
973.694.6274

WEST ORANGE
Rabbi Efraim Mintz
Rabbi Mendy Kasowitz
973.731.0770

WOODCLIFF LAKE
Rabbi Dov Drizin
201.476.0157

NEW MEXICO
SANTA FE
Rabbi Berel Levertov
505.983.2000

NEW YORK
ALBANY
Rabbi Yossi Rubin
518.482.5781

ARMONK, CHAPPAQUA, & PLEASANTVILLE
Rabbi Yosef Y. Butman
914.273 9770

BEDFORD
Rabbi Arik Wolf
914.666.6065

BINGHAMTON
Mrs. Rivkah Slonim
607.797.0015

BRIGHTON BEACH
Rabbi Zushe Winner
Rabbi Avrohom Winner
718.946.9833

BROOKLYN HEIGHTS
Rabbi Aaron Raskin
718.596.4840 X11

BUFFALO
Rabbi Moshe Gurary
716.578.1136

CEDARHURST
Rabbi Shneur Zalman Wolowik
516.295.2478

DIX HILLS
Rabbi Yaakov Saacks
631.351.8672

DOBBS FERRY
Rabbi Benjy Silverman
914.693.6100

FOREST HILLS
Rabbi Eli Blokh
Rabbi Yossi Mendelson
718.459.8432 X17

GLEN HEAD
Rabbi Mendy Heber
516.671.6620

ITHACA
Rabbi Eli Silberstein
607.257.7379

KINGSTON
Rabbi Yitzchok Hecht
845.334.9044

LARCHMONT
Rabbi Mendel Silberstein
914.834.4321

LONG ISLAND CITY
Rabbi Zev Wineberg
347.277.0023

NYC GRAMERCY PARK
Rabbi Naftali Rotenstreich
212.924.3200

NYC KEHILATH JESHURUN
Rabbi Elie Weinstock
212.774.5636

NYC WASHINGTON SQUARE
Rabbi Yaakov Bankhalter
Rabbi Adam Reiss
212.627.3270

OSSINING
Rabbi Dovid Labkowski
914.923.2522

PORT WASHINGTON
Rabbi Shalom Paltiel
516.767.8672

RIVERDALE
Rabbi Levi Shemtov
718.549.1100

ROCHESTER
Rabbi Nechemia Vogel
585.271.0330

ROSLYN
Rabbi Yaakov Reiter
516.484.8185

SCARSDALE
Rabbi Velvl Butman
914.723.2422

SEA GATE
Rabbi Chaim Brikman
Mrs. Rivka Brikman
718.266.1736

STATEN ISLAND
Rabbi Moshe Katzman
Rabbi Shmuel Bendet
718.370.8953

STONY BROOK
Rabbi Shalom Ber Cohen
631.585.0521

SUFFERN
Rabbi Isaac Lefkowitz
Rabbi Shmuel Gancz
845.368.1889

WOODBURY
Rabbi Shmuel Lipszyc
516.682.0404

NORTH CAROLINA
ASHEVILLE
Rabbi Shaya Susskind
828.505.0746

CHARLOTTE
Rabbi Yossi Groner
Rabbi Shlomo Cohen
704.366.3984

RALEIGH
Rabbi Aaron Herman
919.637.6950

RALEIGH
Rabbi Pinchas Herman
Rabbi Sholom Ber Estrin
919.847.8986

OHIO
BEACHWOOD
Rabbi Yossi Marosov
216.381.4736

BLUE ASH
Rabbi Yisroel Mangel
513.793.5200

COLUMBUS
Rabbi Areyah Kaltmann
Rabbi Levi Andrusier
614.294.3296

DAYTON
Rabbi Nochum Mangel
Rabbi Dr. Shmuel Klatzkin
937.643.0770

TOLEDO
Rabbi Yossi Shemtov
419.843.9393

OKLAHOMA
OKLAHOMA CITY
Rabbi Ovadia Goldman
405.524.4800

TULSA
Rabbi Yehuda Weg
918.492.4499

OREGON
PORTLAND
Rabbi Moshe Wilhelm
Rabbi Mordechai Wilhelm
503.977.9947

PENNSYLVANIA
AMBLER
Rabbi Shaya Deitsch
215.591.9310

BALA CYNWYD
Rabbi Shraga Sherman
610.660.9192

CLARKS SUMMIT
Rabbi Benny Rapoport
570.587.3300

DEVON
Rabbi Yossi Kaplan
610.971.9977

DOYLESTOWN
Rabbi Mendel Prus
215.340.1303

FOX CHAPEL
Rabbi Ely Rosenfeld
412.781.1800

LANCASTER
Rabbi Elazar Green
717.368.6565

NEWTOWN
Rabbi Aryeh Weinstein
215.497.9925

PHILADELPHIA: CENTER CITY
Rabbi Yochonon Goldman
215.238.2100

PITTSBURGH
Rabbi Yisroel Altein
412.422.7300 ext. 269

PITTSBURGH: SOUTH HILLS
Rabbi Mendy Rosenblum
412.278.3693

RYDAL
Rabbi Zushe Gurevitz
215.572.1511

SHADYSIDE
Rabbi Mordy Rudolph
412.363.2422

RHODE ISLAND
BARRINGTON
Rabbi Moshe Laufer
401.273.7238

SOUTH CAROLINA
COLUMBIA
Rabbi Hesh Epstein
803.782.1831

TENNESSEE
BELLEVUE
Rabbi Yitzchok Tiechtel
615.646.5750

MEMPHIS
Rabbi Levi Klein
901.766.1800

TEXAS
DALLAS
Rabbi Zvi Drizin
972.818.0770

FORT WORTH
Rabbi Dov Mandel
817.361.7704

HOUSTON
Rabbi Moishe Traxler
Rabbi Dovid Goldstein
713.774.0300

HOUSTON: RICE UNIVERSITY AREA
Rabbi Eliezer Lazaroff
Rabbi Yitzchok Schmukler
713.522.2004

PLANO
Rabbi Mendel Block
Rabbi Yehudah Horowitz
972.596.8270

S. ANTONIO
Rabbi Chaim Block
Rabbi Yossi Marrus
210.492.1085

UTAH
SALT LAKE CITY
Rabbi Benny Zippel
801.467.7777

VIRGINIA
ALEXANDRIA/ARLINGTON
Rabbi Mordechai Newman
703.370.2774

FAIRFAX
Rabbi Leibel Fajnland
703.426.1980

NORFOLK
Rabbi Aaron Margolin
Rabbi Levi Brashevitzky
757.616.0770

RICHMOND
Rabbi Dr. Shlomo Pereira
804.740.2000

TYSONS CORNER
Rabbi Levi Deitsch
703.356.3451

WASHINGTON
BELLEVUE
Rabbi Mordechai Farkash
Rabbi Sholom Elishevitz
425.957.7860

SEATTLE
Rabbi Elazar Bogomilsky
206.527.1411

WISCONSIN
MEQUON
Rabbi Menachem Rapoport
262.242.2235

MILWAUKEE
Rabbi Mendel Shmotkin
Rabbi Shais Taub
414.961.6100

AUSTRALIA
Brisbane
Rabbi Chanoch Sufrin
617.3843.6770

Melbourne
Rabbi Shimshon Yurkowicz
613.9822.3600

Perth
Rabbi Shalom White
618.9275.2106

Sydney
Bondi
Rabbi Pinchas Feldman
612.9387.3822

Double Bay
Rabbi Yanky Berger
612.9327.1644

Dover Heights
Rabbi Benzion Milecki
612.9337.6775

North Shore
Rabbi Nochum Schapiro
Mrs. Fruma Schapiro
Rabbi Shmuly Kopel
612.9488.9548

AUSTRIA
Vienna
Rabbi Shaya Boas
431.369.1818 ext. 123

BELGIUM
Antwerp
Rabbi Mendy Gurary
32.3.239.6212

BRAZIL
S. Paulo
Rabbi Avraham Steinmetz
55.11.3081.3081

CANADA
ALBERTA
Calgary
Rabbi Mordechai Groner
403.238.4880

BRITISH COLUMBIA
Richmond
Rabbi Yechiel Baitelman
604.277.6427

Victoria
Rabbi Meir Kaplan
250.595.7656

MANITOBA
Winnipeg
Rabbi Avrohom Altein
Rabbi Shmuel Altein
204.339.8737

ONTARIO
London
Rabbi Eliezer Gurkow
519.434.3962

Ottawa
Rabbi Menachem M. Blum
613.823.0866

Greater Toronto
Regional Office & Thornhill
Rabbi Yossi Gansburg
905.731.7000
Lawrence/Eglinton
Rabbi Menachem Gansburg
416.546.8770

Markham
Rabbi Avraham E. Plotkin
905.886.0420

Midtown
Rabbi Shlomo Wolvovsky
416.516.2005

Mississauga
Rabbi Yitzchok Slavin
905.820.4432

Richmond Hill
Rabbi Mendel Bernstein
905.770.7700

Uptown
Rabbi Moshe Steiner
647.267.8533

York University
Rabbi Vidal Bekerman
416.856.4575

QUEBEC
Montreal
Rabbi Berel Bell
Rabbi Ronnie Fine
Rabbi Leibel Fine
514.342.3.JLI

Town of Mount Royal
Rabbi Moshe Krasnanski
514.739.0770

COLOMBIA
Bogota
Rabbi Yehoshua B. Rosenfeld
Rabbi Chanoch Piekarski
571.635.8251

DENMARK
Copenhagen
Rabbi Yitzchok Lowenthal
45.3316.1850

GREECE
Athens
Rabbi Mendel Hendel
30.210.520.2880

GUATEMALA
Guatemala City
Rabbi Shalom Pelman
502.2485.0770

FINLAND
Helsinki
Rabbi Benyamin Wolff
358.9.278.1770

NETHERLANDS
Den Haag
Rabbi Shmuel Katzman
31.70.347.0222

Rotterdam
Rabbi Yehuda Vorst
31.10.466.9481

PUERTO RICO
Carolina
Rabbi Mendel Zarchi
787.253.0894

RUSSIA
Moscow
Rabbi Shneor Leider
Rabbi Yanky Klein
749.5783.8479

SINGAPORE
Singapore
Rabbi Mordechai Abergel
656.337.2189

SOUTH AFRICA
Cape Town
Rabbi Mendel Popack
Rabbi Pinchas Hecht
27.21.434.3740

Johannesburg
Rabbi Dovid Masinter
Rabbi Yossi Hecht
Rabbi Daniel Rabin
27.11.440.6600

SWEDEN
Stockholm
Rabbi Chaim Greisman
468.679.7067

UNITED KINGDOM
London
Rabbi Gershon Overlander
Rabbi Dovid Katz
502.2485.0770

Leeds
Rabbi Eli Pink
44.113.266.3311

URUGUAY
Montevideo
Rabbi Eliezer Shemtov
5982.709.3444 ext. 109/110

VENEZUELA
Caracas
Rabbi Yehoshua Rosenblum
58.212.264.7011

NOTES

NOTES